W9-BOB-275

Benjamin W. Griffith, Ph.D.,
Emeritus Professor of English
West Georgia College

English Literature

BARRON'S

© Copyright 1991 by Barron's Educational Series, Inc.

All rights reserved.
No part of this book may be reproduced in any form, by
photostat, microfilm, xerography, or any other means, or
incorporated into any information retrieval system, electronic
or mechanical, without the written permission of the
copyright owner.

All inquiries should be addressed to:
Barron's Educational Series, Inc.
250 Wireless Boulevard
Hauppauge, New York 11788

Library of Congress Catalog Card No. 91-8075

ISBN-13: 978-0-8120-4600-7
ISBN-10: 0-8120-4600-5

Library of Congress Cataloging-in-Publication Data
Griffith, Benjamin W.
  Study keys to English literature / by Benjamin Griffith.
    p.   cm.—(Barron's study keys)
  Includes index.
  ISBN 0-8120-4600-5
  1. English literature—Outlines, syllabi, etc.   I. Title.
  II. Series.
PR87.G73   1991
820.9—dc20   91-8075
                                                 CIP

PRINTED IN CHINA

15 14 13

CONTENTS

Theme 1 ANCIENT BRITAIN

*M*any literary historians use the term "Middle Ages" to describe a period in English literature that encompasses 800 years, from Caedmon's *Hymn* at the end of the 7th century to the morality play *Everyman* at the beginning of the 16th century. There are many striking differences, however, between the periods before and after the conquest of the island by the Normans in 1066. There were radical changes in English culture and literature, as well as an emerging new English language after 1066. The prior period can better be designated as the era of Ancient Britain, a time in which a Germanic "Old English" was spoken and a culture brought by the Angles, Saxons, and Jutes from the Continent was being assimilated by the Celts and other native Britons.

INDIVIDUAL KEYS IN THIS THEME

1	Cultural backgrounds of ancient British literature
2	The Old English language
3	Old English poetry
4	*Beowulf*
5	Old English Christian poetry
6	Alfred and the beginning of English prose

Key 1   Cultural backgrounds of ancient British literature

OVERVIEW   *Many cultures and ethnic groups were in conflict in Ancient Britain. The Romans, Germanic invaders, and Christian missionaries brought a diverse mix of culture to the Celtic tribes who occupied the island.*

Roman influence: Beginning in 43 A.D., the island became a part of the Roman Empire. Impressive roads were built, towns flourished, peace was kept under Roman law, and the invaders and Celtic Britons intermarried.

Northern European invaders: Soon after the Roman legions withdrew in the early fifth century, Romanized Britain was in conflict with the isolated Celtic tribes from present-day Scotland and Wales. The Angles, Saxons, and Jutes (Germanic tribes from western Europe, generally called Anglo-Saxons) invaded amid this turmoil and eventually conquered the island.

Social classes: The militant Anglo-Saxon culture had two classes: the ruling class, called **earls**, and the lower class, called **churls** (or bondsmen). Society was organized by families and clans.

Royalty: There was a concept of unquestioned loyalty to tribesmen and to the king, ideally a revered leader, hero, and a wise judge who gave rewards to loyal warriors. Wars and famines caused problems, but everyone could depend wholly on the courage and loyalty of fellow tribesmen.

Anglo-Saxon religion: Many deities were worshiped, all having special strengths and virtues found in nature or in animals. Immortality was believed to come from dying in battle; destiny was controlled by **wyrd** (or fate).

Coming of Christianity: The monk Augustine arrived in Kent in 597 and converted King Ethelbert. Within two generations, Christianity had spread throughout Britain. Monks began teaching Latin and Greek classics in monastery schools, and when Alfred was crowned in 871, he ordered important classics translated into West Saxon.

Importance of Old English literature: After suffering centuries of neglect, Old English literature is now thought to be the greatest Germanic literature of its time.

Key 2 The Old English language

OVERVIEW *The English spoken during the six centuries before 1150 differs so markedly from our modern English that it is virtually a foreign language. Old English, spoken from about 450 to 1150, had a complex grammar with a system of word endings (inflections) to indicate word relationships.*

Old English vocabulary: The vocabulary was small and resistant to change, unlike modern English, which incorporates words from many other languages. Quickly apparent to the modern reader is the absence of French and Latin words, which form so large a part of our present vocabulary.

Pronunciation: The Old English word *stān* is the same as modern English *stone*, indicating that the vowels have undergone a change, or "vowel shift." The long *a* vowel is formed further back in the throat than the sound of the long *o*, which is easier to make and therefore was substituted for ease of pronunciation. *Examples: hālig-holy, bānbone, rāp-rope,* and *gān-go.*

KEY EXAMPLES

"Ēadwine eorl cōm mid landfyrde and drāf hine ūt" means "Earl Edwin came with a land army and drove him out."
"Se hālga Andreas him andswarode" translates as "The Holy Andrew answered him."

Dialects: There were great differences among the four major dialects spoken in Anglo-Saxon England: Northumbrian, Mercian, Kentish, and West Saxon. Nearly all of the surviving Old English manuscripts that have literary importance were written in the West Saxon dialect.

Classification of English: The English language is one of the Western Germanic languages and is therefore of the Indo-European family. Languages most like English are Frisian (spoken along the northern coast of Holland) and Low German ("Plattdeutsch"), spoken in northern Germany. The English of today resulted from the fusion of the language of the Germanic tribes who came to England.

Key 3   Old English poetry

OVERVIEW   *Before the coming of Christianity, poems—composed and presented orally—were used to preserve folklore. Most of the early poetry (like* Beowulf *and* The Battle of Maldon*) is concerned with heroic battle feats, but some is lyrical.*

Rhythm: Old English verse has four main emphases (or beats) in each line, reflecting the way these poems were performed to the accompaniment of loud strums on a harp or lyre. *Scops* (or bards), accompanied by a harp or lyre, sang their verse tales to audiences in mead halls.

Kennings: Bards used many traditional phrases, unique figures of speech called *kennings. Examples: swan-rad* ("swan's riding-place") for sea; *hilde-leoma* ("light of battle") for sword; *mere-hraegl* ("sea-garment") for sail; *mere-hengest* ("sea horse") for ship; *ban-haus* ("bone-house") for body; and *woruld-candel* ("world candle") for sun.

Alliteration: The verse was highly alliterative; in a pair of poetic lines, four or five stressed words might begin with the same consonant or vowel. *Examples:* "hu hī faerlice/flet ofgēoton" and "werodes wisa/word-hord onleac."

Repetition: As in Hebraic poetry of the Old Testament, statements are repeated, in differing words, for emphasis.

Rapid narrative style: Unnecessary details are omitted so that the story can move forward unhindered. This is especially true of the epic *Beowulf.*

KEY POEMS

Deor's Lament (c. 500) is a melancholy lyric of a scop who has lost favor with the king and has been replaced.

The Wife's Lament (from Exeter Book, c. 800) is the bitter lyric of a wife who is living with hostile relatives after her husband has been captured in battle.

The Seafarer (from Exeter Book, c. 725) is a doleful monologue by a sailor who is complaining of the cold northern sea and its fearful storms.

Key 4 Beowulf

OVERVIEW   Beowulf, *the epic poem that is the chief surviving monument of Old English literature, was composed in Northumbria, England, about 750 A.D. It was intended to be sung by a **scop** to entertain eighth-century audiences.*

The anonymous author: The poem was eventually written down about the year 1000 in Wessex by an Anglo-Saxon who had training in the church, who understood the royal court, who knew the folklore, and who had a good command of the techniques of Anglo-Saxon poetry. There are many allusions to the Bible: God is said to be the creator of all things, the monster Grendel is called a descendant of Cain, and Hell and the Devil await the villainous monsters. There is also some cultural confusion; the author, for example, seems to equate God's will with the concept of fate (or **wyrd**).

The manuscript: The British Museum contains the only surviving manuscript of *Beowulf*, which fortunately survived a fire in 1731, before any modern transcription had been made of the poem.

Historical evidence: One event in the poem—Hygelac's raid on the Frisians—has been documented in Frankish chronicles as happening between 512 and 520.

Anglo-Saxon culture in *Beowulf*: The poem emphasizes the close relationship between kinsmen, the importance of the relationship between the warrior (**thane**) and his lord, and the devotion to the virtue of courage.

KEY NARRATIVE

A monster named **Grendel** begins raiding Hrothgar's court and killing his thanes. **Beowulf**, a Geat, is summoned to kill the monster, which he does by wrenching off his gigantic arm. Beowulf fights **Grendel's mother**, whom he slays with a magical sword he finds as they struggle in a mysterious hall beneath the ocean. The third story concerns the honoring of Beowulf by Hrothgar and Beowulf's return home. Years later, when he is old, Beowulf is called to battle a dragon, who kills the old hero.

Key 5 Old English Christian poetry

OVERVIEW *Old English poetry, composed orally before the Christian era and amended by the monks who put it into manuscript form, combines pagan mythology and Christian symbols. In* The Dream of the Rood, *for example, Christ is described as a "young hero . . . strong and stout-hearted."*

The poet Caedmon: The Venerable Bede, in his *Ecclesiastical History of the British Nation* (731), tells how verse was composed by a remarkable poet named Caedmon, an uneducated herdsman. In his village the harp was passed around at evening meals, and impromptu songs were composed. Each time Caedmon saw the harp approaching, he would leave the table in embarrassment, feeling unable to contribute. One night in a dream he was directed to compose a poem about the Creation, and he was able to remember the entire poem when he awoke.

Caedmon's Hymn: The only surviving poem definitely attributed to Caedmon is a nine-line one known as *Caedmon's Hymn.* Its subject is the Creation, and it contains the line (translated into modern English): "We should sing how he, the eternal Lord, set up a beginning to every wondrous thing."

Other poems ascribed to Caedmon: The Junius Manuscripts (c. 950) contain poems with biblical subjects that Bede has connected with Caedmon.
- **Genesis** alliteratively paraphrases the first 22 chapters of the Old Testament.
- **Judith** is a fragmentary poem about the beheading of an Assyrian commander by the lovely widow Judith.
- **Exodus** paraphrases the story of the Israelites passing through the Red Sea.

The poet Cynewulf (c. 750–c. 825): Ranked second only to the poet who wrote *Beowulf*, **Cynewulf** is best known for *Dream of the Rood*, a poem about the Crucifixion as told by the Cross itself. Because of its tenderness and imaginativeness, it is considered the finest of the Old English religious poems.

Key 6 Alfred and the beginning of English prose

OVERVIEW *King Alfred the Great (849–c. 900) saw the need for educating his people and translated Latin works into the language actually used by the people: Old English.*

Alfred's importance: He wrote prefaces for his various translations and added explanations and expansions of the text. For this he is called the "Father of English prose." He is also credited with preserving most of the surviving Old English literature.

Alfred's translations: This intellectual Anglo-Saxon monarch translated four of the most significant works of his time: Pope Gregory's "Pastoral Care," Paulus Orosius's "Universal History," the Venerable Bede's "Ecclesiastical History," and Boethius's "Concerning the Consolation of Philosophy."

The Anglo-Saxon Chronicle: Probably initiated about 891 at Alfred's direction, this history of England from the invasion of Julius Caesar through 891 is the first original narrative prose in the people's vernacular language anywhere in the western world. No other people at that time had such a complete history in the language the people actually spoke.

Poems from *The Anglo-Saxon Chronicle:* "The Battle of Brunanburh" is a fervent patriotic poem celebrating an English victory. "The Battle of Maldon" is an excellent poetic description of brave Anglo-Saxon warriors driving back Norse invaders. Some critics judge it to be a finer pure epic poem than *Beowulf,* particularly in its characterization of the giant leader, Alderman Byrhthoth, whose skeleton, when exhumed in 1769, measured six feet nine inches in length.

Aelfric (c. 955–c. 1020): Educated under Alfred's direction, Aelfric was a gifted prose writer whose works include sermons, translations from the Old Testament, and texts on grammar and mathematics.

Wulfstan (d. 1023): Fifty-three sermons have been attributed to Wulfstan. His best known, "Wolf's Sermon to the English" (1014), is written in forceful, elegant Old English prose. In it he states that the raids by the Vikings are in retribution for English sins.

Theme 2 MEDIEVAL ENGLAND

*A*fter the Norman Conquest the English language was no longer used by the aristocracy, who embraced the French dialect of their Norman conquerors. English survived and developed, however, through its use among the lower and middle classes. In the 13th and 14th centuries the most popular literary works for the anti-aristocratic audiences were medieval romances, in which the heroic knights behaved in the crudest fashion as they ate, fought, or made love. The most important event was the flowering in the late 14th century of three great poets: the so-called "Pearl Poet," William Langland, and Geoffrey Chaucer.

INDIVIDUAL KEYS IN THIS THEME

Key 7 Cultural backgrounds of Medieval English literature

OVERVIEW *The Middle Ages are sometimes referred to as the "Dark Ages," obscuring the many cultural changes that took place in language, literature, the arts, and even the political and class structures.*

Language: After the Norman Conquest, when aristocrats embraced the Norman French dialect, literary works were written in Latin or French. It was not until early in the 14th century that English again emerged as a literary and political language. In the mouths of ordinary citizens, English became richer; more than 10,000 French words were added, and principles were established that made English evolve in ever-freer adaptations.

Architecture: Although little great literature was written in English during the three centuries after 1066, there was one crowning artistic achievement: the completing of the 27 great cathedrals of England. Such unity of devotion and effort has rarely been equaled. With a small population for support, 16 of the cathedrals were started between 1070 and 1100; all were essentially complete by 1350.

The powerful Church: In Norman England the Church became increasingly strong, as evidenced by the construction of cathedrals. Through the Church, the culture of Greece and Rome was disseminated, manuscripts copied, and universities established at Cambridge and Oxford. In medieval thought, the Church and the King were "the two swords of God" in maintaining order in society.

Nationalism: Partly due to the war with France, the English began to take a nationalistic pride in their country and their language in the 14th century. English instead of French was taught regularly in schools.

Social structure: By 1250 the steady growth of trade and industry led to a rising middle class, with guilds to protect members who practiced crafts and trades. The plague reduced the labor force and led to higher wages and to the demands of the Peasants' Revolt in 1381. Chaucer, in his *Canterbury Tales,* brilliantly depicts the varied social strata.

Key 8   Middle English as a language

OVERVIEW   *In the year 1000 the opening words of the Lord's Prayer were written in Old English: "Faeder ure thu eart on heofunum, si thin nama gehalgod." In* The Wycliffe Bible *(1389), it begins: "Oure fadir that art in hevenes, halwid be thi name." English thus made a giant stride from its Germanic heritage toward the language as we speak it today.*

Principal differences between Old and Middle English: The grammar was simplified and the vocabulary greatly enlarged.
- The **inflections** (special word endings showing relationships between sentence parts) virtually disappear in Middle English.
- The **word order** in Chaucer's time was like that of Modern English, with the subject coming before the predicate and the modifier before the word modified. *Example:* "oure fadir," not "Faeder ure."
- The **vocabulary** of Old English was primarily Germanic, but Middle English was enriched by borrowed words.
- Middle English **spelling** is less uniform because it incorporates several regional dialects, each with its own system of representing sounds in writing.
- The **"natural gender"** evolved in Middle English. We uniformly refer to male beings as masculine, female ones as feminine, unlike other European languages.
- The **pronunciation** of Old English guttural sounds was softened in Middle English, but with no consistent system, leading to varied pronunciations of words with the same ending. *Examples:* plough, hiccough, rough, cough, though, and slough.

English in the barn, French in the kitchen: In Sir Walter Scott's novel *Ivanhoe,* the character Wamba notes that although *cow, sheep, pig,* and *deer* are words from Old English, culinary words such as *beef, veal, mutton, pork, bacon,* and *venison* are derived from French. The reason is that ladies speaking Norman French gave orders to the kitchen staff, and thus these words for meat were added to the cook's vocabulary. Herdsmen continued to use the English words for animals on the hoof. This illustrates the distinction in modern English, in which words relating to culture, government, and "polite" terms generally have French or Latin roots while the "little words of house and home" derive from Anglo-Saxon roots.

Key 9   The importance of *The Wycliffe Bible*

OVERVIEW   *John Wycliffe (c. 1328–84) was an Oxford theologian and religious reformer whose writings championed the poor, who he thought were overburdened by the power of the Church. He encouraged the first translation of the Bible into English so that persons could interpret the Scriptures individually.*

The Lollard movement: Wycliffe attacked the Church's power in his sermons and other writings, advocating that the state take over the vast landholdings of the Church. More practically, he sent out simple, devoted men, called Lollards, to preach to people in their native tongue, revealing the living truths of religion which they said the formalism of church had obscured. The Lollards identified with the poor, wearing coarse russet robes and carrying staves. Many of them were executed in the fourth quarter of the 14th century.

Links with literature: Although Chaucer's works contain only one reference to the peasant uprising and one to the Lollards, the tone of Chaucer's *Canterbury Tales* and his satiric thrusts at the land-hungry power of the medieval church owes much to Wycliffe's movement.

Links with history: Perhaps unintentionally, Wycliffe's Lollard movement helped instigate the Peasant's Revolt of 1381. His efforts to remove the Church from political and materialistic concerns were part of the movement that led to the Reformation.

The Wycliffe Bible: In two versions, c. 1382 and c. 1395, this was the earliest complete translation of the Bible into English. Some scholars claim that none of the actual translation was done by Wycliffe; it is most probably the work of Nicholas of Hereford and John Purvey, encouraged by Wycliffe. The **King James Version of the Bible** (Key 24), which had more influence on English literature than any other book, made extensive use of *The Wycliffe Bible*.

Links with the language: Wycliffe and his associates, in translating the Bible, are credited with incorporating more than a thousand Latin words not found previously in English.

Key 10   The alliterative revival in Medieval poetry

OVERVIEW   *Between 1350 and 1400, over twenty significant Middle English poems in the alliterative style of Old English poetry were written.*

Characteristics: Unlike the works of Chaucer, these poems seem written to be recited, show little of the personality of the author, use myths and conventional subjects, and seek to teach a lesson, usually through allegory.

The Pearl Poet: The authorship of several anonymous alliterative poems in similar style, diction, and dialect have been attributed to the "Pearl Poet."

- *Pearl* is a dream allegory lamenting the death of the poet's two-year-old daughter and envisioning Paradise.

- *Purity* (or *Cleanness*) promotes the virtue of purity by paraphrasing Biblical stories of the Flood, the destruction of Sodom and Gomorrah, and the fall of Belshazzer in passages of great power.

- *Patience* illustrates the evils of impatience by retelling the story of Jonah in a humorous way, complete with a realistic picture of the whale's interior.

Sir Gawain and the Green Knight: This elegantly constructed, vivid narrative poem, attributed by some to the Pearl Poet, is one of the greatly admired works of medieval literature. The narrative is divided into four parts, or *fitts*:

- **The Challenge:** The giant Green Knight appears in King Arthur's court on New Year's Day, daring anyone to chop off his head and receive a similar stroke a year and a day hence. Gawain accepts the challenge and severs the head of the giant, who picks up his head and dashes away.

- **The Knightly Quest:** Gawain sets out to fulfill his pledge, but loses his way and comes to a castle where he is welcomed by the lord, his beautiful lady, and a hideous old hag. The host plans three days of pleasant activity; the two lords vow to exchange each night tokens won during the day.

- **The Temptation:** The lady forces her attentions on Gawain, kissing him. When the lord returns from the hunt, Gawain receives that day's kill and responds with a kiss. On the second day he receives and exchanges two kisses, on the third, three. But Gawain withholds another gift from the lady: a magic green baldric (belt) that is supposed to preserve the wearer's life.
- **The Return Blow:** When Gawain faces the Green Knight on New Year's Day, he flinches from the first two blows and sustains a slight gash on the neck from the third. Then he learns that the Green Knight is really his generous host and that the old hag is Arthur's fairy sister, Morgan-Le-Fay, who had devised this strategy to corrupt Gawain and shame King Arthur's court.

Medieval Meaning of *Gawain*: This allegory, intended to teach the virtues of chivalry and knighthood, may be associated with the founding of England's Order of the Garter. Except for his weakness in the baldric episode, Gawain's behavior is above reproach.

Piers Plowman: More than sixty manuscripts survive in three differing versions of *Piers Plowman,* attesting to the popularity of this alliterative poem, the full title of which is *The Vision of William Concerning Piers the Plowman.* Notes in certain manuscripts ascribe the authorship to a William Langland. In form it is a dream-vision, one of the most common of medieval literary devices. It is considered by many to be the greatest poem of the Middle English Alliterative Revival.
- **Basic content:** The poet dreams of a tower on a hill, a dungeon in the valley, and a "fair field full of folk" in between. Symbolically, God lives in the tower, the devil in the dungeon. In the so-called B-text of the poem, there are eight separate visions, described by a narrator called Will. The themes are primarily religious, and the poem ends with Conscience setting out to find Piers, who will lead them, it is hoped, on a perfected search for Salvation.
- **Importance of the poem:** It is second only to the *Canterbury Tales* in giving vivid scenes of medieval life that depict a famine, the evils of gluttony, and the greed of unscrupulous landlords, officials, friars, lawyers, and merchants. The tone is satirical and angry, but in the words of a sincere and religious common man. Many of the sayings in *Piers Plowman* became slogans shouted by the protesters in the Peasants' Revolt.

Key 11 Chaucer and his works

OVERVIEW *Geoffrey Chaucer (1340–1400) served three English kings in high governmental positions; concurrently, he wrote an extraordinary body of poetry that touched all phases of English life and art.*

Works: Traditionally, Chaucer's literary career has been divided into three periods that reflect the influences and styles that affected his writing.

- **French period:** Chaucer followed French poetic conventions in the allegorical elegy, *The Book of the Duchess* (1369), and *The Parliament of Fowls*, a St. Valentine's Day poem celebrating a royal betrothal. He also translated into English poetry the *Roman de la Rose,* the most popular and influential of all French poems in the Middle Ages.

- **Italian period:** Visiting Italy on diplomatic missions, Chaucer was influenced to write *Troilus and Cressida,* his longest complete poem, largely adapted from Boccaccio's story *Filostrato* (The Love-Stricken One). Other poems colored by Italian reminiscences are a dream allegory, *The House of Fame,* and *The Legend of Good Women,* a collection of stories in heroic couplets about famous women of antiquity who were faithful in love.

- **English period:** Here Chaucer adds an important ingredient to the conventional artistry of the earlier periods: his unique personality. In the *Canterbury Tales* he describes, with a tolerant humor and restrained wit, nearly every type of person found in medieval England in various classes, trades, and professions.

The *Canterbury Tales*: Chaucer's most celebrated work, it contains about 17,000 lines in prose and verse of various meters (though primarily in rhymed couplets).

- **The plan:** Chaucer originally conceived a framing device with a motley company of thirty travelers telling two stories each way on their pilgrimage to Canterbury and return to London. The design was similar to Boccaccio's *Decameron,* in which stories were told by a group sequestered from the plague. Chaucer began the work about 1386, but only twenty-four stories (four of these unfinished) had been written when he died in 1400.

- **The General Prologue:** An important poem in its own right, it describes the meeting of 29 pilgrims at the Tabard Inn in Southwark (now a part of London). In fact, the pilgrims add up to 31 in the Prologue, and 21 of them are described colorfully in brief word pictures that reveal their personalities, dress, and even the kind of horse they ride.

- **Sources:** Not original with Chaucer, but freely adapted from works well known in the Middle Ages, the stories include every type of medieval fiction as well as a sermon.
- **The characters:** The brilliance of Chaucer's art is shown in his creation of a marvelously varied portrait gallery of medieval characters, both in and out of the Church. Forever memorable are the Wife of Bath, a free-wheeling feminist figure; the "poor Parson," the only churchman Chaucer approves of; the Miller, a coarse and quarrelsome bully; the Prioress, a dainty and pretentious prig; and an assortment of unlikely and roundly satirized prelates: the Monk, the Summoner, and the Friar.

KEY TALES

"The Miller's Tale" is a ribald story of the conning of a husband, through the expectation of a second Flood, and a lover, who expects to kiss a lady's lips, but is offered her "nether eye."

"The Reeve's Tale" is a fabliau about two clerks, having been robbed by a miller, taking revenge by sleeping with his wife and daughter.

"The Wife of Bath's Tale" offers a rapist-knight freedom if he answers the question, "What do women most desire?" The "loathly lady" who gives him the answer (women want to have their own way) is transformed into a beautiful wife.

"The Clerk's Tale" tells of patient and obedient Griselda, who withstands the trials meted out by a relentless husband.

"The Merchant's Tale" is the story of an old man married to a young wife. When he goes blind, she makes love in a pear tree with a young lover, during which event Pluto mischievously restores the old man's sight.

"The Pardoner's Tale" is a sermon as well as a story of three riotous young men who set out to find Death and destroy him. Instead, their greed destroys them.

"The Nun's Priest's Tale" is a beast fable about a cock who is flattered and caught by a fox, who in turn is flattered by the cock, who escapes.

Key 12   The prose of Sir Thomas
Malory

OVERVIEW   *Malory's* Morte Darthur, *a gathering of the main body of legends about King Arthur into one narrative, is the best-known work of fifteenth-century English literature.*

Influence: Malory's simple, forthright telling of the Arthurian lore is still enjoyed by modern readers, and the work has long inspired other writings, such as Tennyson's *Idylls of the King*.

Malory's reputation—myth or fact? For many years scholars have identified the author of *Morte Darthur* with a Warwickshire knight who was charged with extortion, robbery, and rape and who spent the last twenty years of his life in prison. Recent investigations have discovered other Thomas Malorys, indicating that the actual author may not have had a criminal record.

Sources of *Morte Darthur:* Malory used 13th century French versions of Arthurian legends, skillfully condensing and rewriting them. Another source was a medieval alliterative poem in English called *Morte Arthure*. Malory omitted minor episodes found in these sources.

Malory's prose style: The conversion of the wordy, long-winded French originals into short, firm sentences with a natural rhythm of speech gives Malory's work its greatest distinction. A blunt, practical man of action who admired knighthood but did not romanticize it, he presented the Arthurian material in a work uniquely his own.

Caxton's edition of *Morte Darthur:* William Caxton (1422?-1491?) introduced printing to England; among his most famous publications are the *Canterbury Tales* and Malory's *Morte Darthur*, published in 1485.

The content of Malory's cycle: A manuscript discovered in 1934 of Malory's work lists the eight principal bodies of Arthurian lore: 1. The Tale of Arthur and Lucius; 2. The Book of King Arthur; 3. The Tale of Sir Lancelot du Lake; 4. Sir Gareth of Orkney; 5. Tristram de Lyones; 6. The quest of the Holy Grail; 7. Lancelot and Guinevere; and 8. The Morte Darthur (death of Arthur).

Key 13 The beginnings of English drama

OVERVIEW *It is ironical that the flourishing drama of Greece and Rome was banned by the early Christian church, while in England priests of the Church acted out biblical scenes and fostered the beginning of drama as we know it today.*

Early drama in the church: In a late 10th-century manuscript, Ethelwold, Bishop of Winchester, instructed Benedictine monks in performing an Easter drama called the *Quem Quaeritis Trope.* The phrase "Quem quaeritis" means "Whom seek ye?" and was asked of the three Marys as they came to the tomb of Jesus. Two members of the church choir, dressed in white as angels, asked the question of three others dressed in black, representing the Marys. Thus English drama was born. Later, a Christmas playlet about the coming of the Magi, *Officium Stellae,* was added to the repertoire.

Church drama becomes popular: The people clamored for more dramatic presentations, and the clergy complied, erecting platforms along the interior walls of the church so that scenes ranging from Creation to Judgment Day could be presented. With no chairs or pews in medieval churches, the crowds could cluster close to the action. The actor-priests began wearing costumes and speaking their lines in vernacular English rather than Latin, receiving the delighted applause of the audiences. Two of the earliest of such dramas in English were *Jacob and Esau* (early 13th century) and *The Harrowing of Hell* (mid-13th century).

Drama moves outside the church: As the dramas placed more strain on the services and the audiences became more unruly, the plays were moved outside, first to the church porch and then to the surrounding grounds and graveyards. The laughter and the excited squeals now greatly increased, and such plays as one in which Noah's wife is a comical drunken shrew became widely popular. The actors began overplaying their roles, to the delight of the simple folk in the audience. By the end of the 13th century the exasperated church banished all dramas from holy ground.

Key 14 Mystery and miracle plays

OVERVIEW *As the 14th century began, drama was free of Church control, and plays were performed by lay persons from the craft guilds which were called "mysteries." To satisfy the growing public demand, the guilds constructed elaborate pageant wagons as stages for their cycles of plays.*

Content: The subject matter was still religious; **mystery plays** (based on the Bible) and **miracle plays** (based upon the lives of saints) were the only dramatic fare.

Cycles of plays: To celebrate Corpus Christi Day, craft guilds presented plays to crowds that remained in place as the pageant wagons rolled to each station. Appropriately, the goldsmith guild performed the Three Wise Men Bearing Gifts; the carpenters, Noah's Ark; and the bakers and brewers, the Last Supper.

Surviving cycles: Although these cycles were performed in about 125 British communities in the 14th and 15th centuries, manuscripts of complete cycles survive only from Chester, York, Wakefield, and the unknown "N. Town."

- **The York Cycle:** The most extensive English cycle, with 48 plays surviving, covers biblical history from the Creation to the Crucifixion.
- **The Wakefield Cycle**: These plays by the so-called "Wakefield Master" are unique in medieval drama. They contain exciting religious theater combined with boisterous humor and high spirits. The best example is the *Second Shepherd's Play*, in which Mak tries to steal a sheep and conceal it in a cradle as a new-born baby. The play satirizes shrewish wives and the overtaxing of the poor. After Mak's guilt is farcically revealed, the other shepherds go to kneel before the new-born Jesus.
- **The Chester Cycle**: Twenty-four "pageants" are included in this cycle, treating sacred history more humorously than in the York cycle, but less so than in the Wakefield. A typical Chester play is one with slapstick humor involving Noah's wife's drunkenness. The Chester plays used an "expositor," who accompanied the pageant wagon on horseback and explained the meaning of the play.

Key 15   The morality plays

OVERVIEW   *The morality plays were allegorical sermons with simple plots, using characters to personify such abstractions as Beauty, Gluttony, Virtue, and Vice. Professional actors were used to perform these plays.*

Everyman (c.1470): In the best known of the morality plays, the character Everyman (representing all humankind) is summoned by Death to the day of judgment. Everyman tries to find a companion for his journey, but all forsake him. Only Good Deeds goes with him into the grave and helps present his case. The play is intensely dramatic as Everyman is deserted by Fellowship, Kindred, Goods, etc. and becomes increasingly terrified.

The Castle of Perseverance (c.1425): This oldest complete morality play has a plot similar to that of *Everyman*. The Bad Angel and Good Angel struggle for the soul of man, and the latter places him in the Castle of Perseverance. Hell's forces cannot prevail against the Castle, but Greed lures him outside, where he dies repentant. Mercy, Peace, Truth, and Righteousness compete in a debate for the man's soul; Mercy wins.

Mankind (c.1475): In this unusual comic morality play, the vices compete for the soul of man, delighting medieval audiences with their lewd antics. Titivullus, a devil who collects words mumbled or skipped in divine services, was a favorite medieval character. He seduces Mankind from Mercy at first, but Mercy triumphs at last.

Magnyfycence (1516): This is the earliest English drama whose authorship is certain. Written by John Skelton (c.1460–1529), it depicts mankind being deceived by vices, but later redeemed by the virtues of Goodhope and Perseverance.

Ane Pleasant Satire of the Thrie Estaitis (1540): Written by Sir David Lindsay, it depicts the temptation of Rex Humanitas by Sensuality, Wantonness, Solace, and other undesirable companions. At the same time, Good Counsel is hurried away, Verity is put in stocks, and Chastity is warned to stay away. Correction arrives to save the day.

Key 16   Middle English lyrics and ballads

OVERVIEW   *Lyrics—short, melodic poems, usually expressing intense personal emotion—are rare in Old English poetry, but are fairly common in medieval literature, with religious lyrics greatly outnumbering secular ones. Ballads—poems that tell stories, often of folk origin—are found in great numbers. Both lyrics and ballads were originally written to be sung.*

Religious lyrics: The extensive cult of the Virgin in the Middle Ages accounts for many songs about the Madonna. The lyric beginning "Lullay, my child, and wepe no more" (usually entitled "A Sacred Lullaby") and "Jesus Christ's Mild Mother" are typical.

Secular lyrics: The best-known lyric in Middle English is *Cuckoo Song* (c.1300), with its joyous outburst in the opening lines; "Sumer is i-cumen in, Lhude sing, cucco!" Also well known is the love lyric "Alysoun" (c.1300), in which the poet praises her fair hair, brown eyes, and "middel smal."

Medieval ballads: Interest in ballads was given a great impetus by the publication of Thomas Percy's *Reliques of Ancient English Poetry* (3 vols., 1765) and Francis James Child's *English and Scottish Popular Ballads* (5 vols., 1882-98). Most ballads treat tragic love, the pagan supernatural, and historical and semi-historical events.
- *Sir Patrick Spens*, an early Scottish ballad, tells of Spens being ordered to sea in winter on a mission for the King. His foreboding of disaster and the tragic drowning of the crew are powerfully and simply told.
- *Barbara Allan*, widely sung in America, tells of Sir John Grehme's dying of unrequited love for Barbara.
- *Tam Lin* tells of Janet winning back to mortal life her elfin lover, Tam, from the queen of the fairies, who had captured him.
- **Robin Hood Cycle of Ballads**: The best-known of this genre is *Robin Hood and Guy of Gisborne*. Robin kills Guy of Gisborne in a deadly fight, disguises himself in Guy's horsehide garment, and tricks the Sheriff of Nottingham.

Theme 3 RENAISSANCE PROSE

*I*n 1485 when Henry VII, the first Tudor monarch, was crowned, an astonishing era of change was beginning. Seven years later, Columbus discovered America, opening the way for the English to colonize the New World. Great cultural changes had recently occurred when William Caxton published the first book in English in 1474. English scholars, called Humanists, visited Italy and brought back the spirit of the Renaissance—a rebirth of literature and art inspired by the rediscovery of classical manuscripts from antiquity. Martin Luther promoted a schism in the Roman Catholic Church in 1517, leading to the Protestant Reformation and England's separation from the Roman Catholic Church. England, under Queen Elizabeth, became strongly nationalistic as Britain gained control of the seas.

Key 17   Characteristics of Renaissance England

OVERVIEW   *The Renaissance (or rebirth of learning), which began in Italy in the 14th century, affected English attitudes toward learning and the arts from approximately 1485, the year of the accession of the Tudor monarchs, to 1660, when Charles II was restored to the throne.*

The new impulse for learning: Before Caxton printed his first book in English, no more than two percent of the English people could read. Afterwards, learning increased rapidly, from the Crown to the commoner: Henry VIII wrote poetry and composed songs; Elizabeth I spoke five foreign languages and encouraged drama and the arts. New schools were founded throughout Britain, in rural villages as well as cities.

Influence of the Humanists: Enlightened by the classics of Greece and Rome, the Humanists emphasized human potential, not God's power, believing one's role in life should be action, not religious contemplation. After the publication of ***The Wycliffe Bible*** (Key 9), Humanists influenced a critical and scholarly study of the scriptures, which partly led to a challenge of Roman Catholicism and the emergence of English Protestantism.

Strong English nationalism: During Queen Elizabeth's reign (1558-1603), England became a world naval power and began the foundations of the far-flung British empire. The defeat of the Spanish Armada in 1588 gave impetus to a powerful surge of nationalistic fervor that energized all English pursuits, including literature and the arts.

KEY RENAISSANCE CHARACTERISTICS
- Emphasis on classical studies in the expanding universities.
- Increasing literacy among the laity.
- Growth of a critical, skeptical type of scholarship, leading to scientific inquiry.
- Increasing trade leads to individual wealth, general prosperity, nationalism, and materialism.
- Gradual movement from unquestioned religious beliefs toward a more human-centered philosophy.

Key 18 The beginnings of modern English

OVERVIEW *English had triumphed over French as the spoken language by the mid-14th century.*

Growth of English: As strong nationalistic feelings developed in England during the Renaissance and the "New Learning" became more scientific and technological, English became the language of scholarship, replacing Latin. With the rise of Protestantism, English became the language of theology; now the English language had no bounds to its development.

Greatly expanded vocabulary: Much growth came from the learned words borrowed from Latin and Greek, but explorers and overseas tradesmen brought an influx of words from many foreign languages.

Willingness to experiment: With such writers as Shakespeare leading the way, new forms of words were invented daily. *Example:* All of the following variants were in actual use in Shakespeare's day: *effectual, effective, effectuating,* and *effectuous.*

Spelling: Early in the Renaissance, spelling was erratic. *Example: Fellow* was spelled *felaw, felowe, fallow,* and *fallowe.* In 1582, Robert Mulcaster proposed as system of regularizing spelling, which was quickly accepted and which had begun to make a noticeable difference by 1600.

Pronunciation: In reading poetic works from the period of Shakespeare, notice that many words are stressed on different syllables from ones currently emphasized. The second syllable was stressed in the following words: *character, illustrate, concentrate,* and *contemplate.*

Changes in grammatical elements:
- **Nouns**: Older plurals like *eyen* and *kine* were replaced by *eyes* and *cows.*
- **Pronouns**: *Ye* was rapidly being replaced by *you,* and *thou, thee,* and *thy* were disappearing from popular speech. The pronoun *its* (not used in the King James Bible) had its first recorded use in 1598.
- **Verbs:** The endings of words like *giveth* and *taketh* changed to *gives* and *takes.*

Key 19   Prose of the Renaissance humanists

OVERVIEW   *The Dutch humanist Desiderius Erasmus (1466?–1536), who came to England during the reign of the first Tudors, stimulated interest in classical writings and exploratory thinking among such English humanists as Sir Thomas More, Sir Thomas Elyot, and Roger Ascham.*

Sir Thomas More (1478–1535): A close friend of Erasmus, More is best known for his prose work *Utopia*, written first in Latin in 1516.

- *Utopia*: Book II, which tells of an ideal state with a truly representative government, is the most widely read. It describes a land where robust health is exalted, work-days are only six hours long, both women and men are educated, all houses are equally comfortable, all religions are tolerated, war is detested, and the welfare of the whole is paramount.

Sir Thomas Elyot (c.1490–1546): He was appointed ambassador to Charles V, Holy Roman Emperor, after writing *The Boke Named the Governour* (1531), the first full work in English on education and moral philosophy. Elyot describes the ideal ruler as a humanist, learned in Greek and Latin, with a body made healthy by the exercise of wrestling and horseback riding. He follows the Renaissance idea that only those in high places, not the masses, should be educated.

Roger Ascham (1515–1568): An accomplished Greek scholar who was tutor to Elizabeth I, Ascham was a master of the distinctly native English prose style.

- *Toxophilus* (1545) is a Platonic dialogue between Philologus (lover of knowledge) and Toxophilus (lover of archery). Of principal interest is the Prologue, where Ascham vigorously urges the use of English as the language of scholars.
- *The Scholemaster* (1570): This treatise on education advocates avoidance of the birch rod on young students. He suggests imitating classical models to develop a good prose style and condemns the *Canterbury Tales* and *Morte Darthur* for immorality.

Key 20 Sidney and Raleigh

OVERVIEW *Sir Philip Sidney (1554–1586) and Sir Walter Raleigh (c. 1552–1618) embodied the ideal Renaissance persona in their versatility; they were courtiers, soldiers, scholars, statesmen, and poets.*

As authors: Raleigh was second only to Sidney among the courtly poets; both were masterly at writing pretty tributes to Queen Elizabeth. They were also accomplished prose writers: Sidney produced literary criticism and fiction, and Raleigh wrote history. Both lived and died dramatically.

The legends of Sidney's death: On September 22, 1586, this Renaissance hero led an attack on a Spanish convoy and received a musket wound in his thigh; he died of infection three weeks later. His friend, Fulke Greville, who was not present at the scene, left two famous embellishments of his death: in one, Sidney left off his thigh armor so that he would not be better protected than the marshal of the camp; in the second, as he was being carried wounded from the field, Sidney saw a dying soldier looking pleadingly at his water bottle and gave it to him with the words, ''Thy necessity is yet greater than mine.'' Sidney was buried in St. Paul's Cathedral.

Sidney's prose: Because of its lush, sensuous language, *The Countess of Pembroke's Arcadia,* a pastoral prose romance, was the most influential prose fiction before *Pilgrim's Progress. The Defence of Poesy* inaugurates English literary criticism. These are two of the most important Renaissance prose works.

- *Arcadia* (1577–85): Written to amuse Sidney's sister, this discursive narrative has two ship-wrecked princes fall in love with the daughters of the King of Arcadia. In romanticized word pictures, Sidney creates a dream world of magical beauty that anticipates Spenser.
- *The Defence of Poesy* (c.1579–84): Sidney defends the writing of imaginative literature against the Puritan charge that it is an enemy of virtue. Sidney argues that poetry has the function of both teaching and delighting. The great end of learning, Sidney wrote, is the living of a virtuous life, and the inspired poet can lead readers to the highest truths.

Sidney's poetry: *Astrophel and Stella* (c. 1580-84), the first true sonnet sequence (or group of related sonnets) in English, established Sidney as the most polished writer of sonnets before Shakespeare. In the sequence, Astrophel (''star lover'') relates his love for Stella (''star'') and celebrates her charms. The 108 sonnets follow the Petrarchan form strictly.

Raleigh's prose: Primarily historical, these reflect the excitement at the expanding of the British Empire from the point of view of a nationalistic Renaissance man.

- *A Report of the Truth of the Fight about the Isles of Acores* (pub. 1591) is a prose epic about the naval battle between Sir Richard Greville's ships against an overwhelming Spanish fleet. Tennyson derived his poem ''The Revenge'' from Raleigh's account.
- *The Discovery of the Large, Rich, and Bewtiful Empire of Guiana* (1596) concerns the quest for gold in a lush, virgin jungle, with graphic accounts of hand-to-hand combat.
- *The History of the World* (1614), written in prison in the Tower of London, contains valuable history (up to 130 B.C.), written in magnificent prose style.

Raleigh's poetry: He is best known for such lyrics as ''The Nymph's Reply to the Shepherd'' (a sardonic reply to Marlowe's idyllic pastoral poem), ''The Lie'' (written from prison), and ''Farewell, False Love,'' (an unconventional lover's complaint, written in vigorous metaphors).

KEY QUOTATION

If all the world and love were young,
And truth in every shepherd's tongue,
These pretty pleasures might me move
To live with thee and be thy love.
                    —Raleigh, from ''The Nymph's Reply to the Shepherd''

Key 21 Elizabethan prose

OVERVIEW *Two types of prose were widely read: fiction, in a genre quite different from modern novels, and chronicles, accounts of travels and historical events.*

John Lyly (1554–1606): His best-known work, *Euphues: The Anatomy of Wit* (1578), was read for its alliterative style and extravagant language rather than its trivial plot and bland moralizing. It was a fad at the court to imitate characters in *Euphues,* asserting "that hot love is soon cold, that the bavin though it burn bright, is but a blaze, that scalding water if it stands a while turneth almost to ice, that pepper though it be hot in the mouth is cold in the maw."

Robert Greene (1500–1592): Also a dramatist, he was the most prolific of the prose fictionists, writing twenty romances in the 1580s, the best-known being *Pandosto, the Triumph of Time* (1588), the source of Shakespeare's *The Winter's Tale.* More significant and distinctive was *A Notable Discovery of Cosenage* (1561), first of a series of "cony-catching" pamphlets about con-men who cheated the innocent. Greene captured accurately the slangy idiom of the underworld.

Thomas Nashe (1567–1601): Nashe's unique tale, *The Unfortunate Traveler, or the Life of Jack Wilton* (1594) is the first **picaresque** novel in English. Picaresque novels describe the adventures of a vagabond or rogue (*picaro* in Spanish) with stark realism.

Raphael Holinshed (d.1580): The *Chronicles of England, Scotland and Ireland* (1578), known as *Holinshed's Chronicles,* is a history of Britain to 1575. From these *Chronicles* Shakespeare borrowed the plot of *Macbeth,* parts of *Cymbeline,* and possibly *King Lear.*

Richard Hakluyt (c.1552–1616): With minor collaboration he wrote the masterpiece of English travel literature: *The Principal Voyages, Traffics, and Discoveries of the English Nation* (3 vols., 1598–1600), which transmits the wonder and novelty of nature in little known parts of the planet Earth.

Samuel Purchas (c.1575–1626): When Hakluyt died, his work was continued by Purchas. The completed work was entitled *Hakluyt's Posthumus,* or *Purchas His Pilgrimes* (1625), which inspired Coleridge to write "Kubla Khan."

Key 22 Literary philosophers: Bacon and Hobbes

OVERVIEW *Previously, British philosophers wrote in Latin, but the 17th Century saw the blossoming of great English philosophical writing. Philosophy was then a type of literature, not a specialized discipline of its own.*

Francis Bacon (1561–1626): A busy public servant and chief adviser to James I, he wrote superb intellectual essays in the Renaissance spirit. He said: "I have taken all knowledge to be my province."
- *Essays* (totaling 106, written 1597–1625): Bacon's primary purpose was to teach young contemporary aristocrats how to succeed. Typical is "Of Riches," which praises wealth and gives advice on attaining it and using it wisely.
- *Advancement of Learning* (1605) is a tract on education in two books; the first praises knowledge and challenges prejudices against learning, the second is a survey of learning, laying a foundation for a national culture.
- *Novum Organum* (1620), the best statement of Bacon's philosophy, espouses the *Novum Organum* ("new instrument") of inductive reasoning to unlock scientific mysteries.

KEY QUOTATIONS

"Some books are to be tasted, others to be swallowed, and some few to be chewed and digested."

"Reading maketh a full man; conference a ready man and writing an exact man."

"Money is like muck, not good except it be spread."

Thomas Hobbes (1588–1679): His philosophical works are considered the major English works of the type between Bacon and Locke.
- *The Elements of Law Natural and Politic* (c.1640) established him as the founder of modern empirical philosophy. He states that the ultimate reality is the ceaseless motion of matter, chief drive is self-preservation, and free will is an illusion.
- *Leviathan* (1651) argues that monarchs rule not by divine right, but because humans, through self-interest, give up natural rights for the security of a strong ruler. A pessimist, he characterized life as "solitary, poor, nasty, brutish, and short."

Key 23   Early 17th Century prose stylists

OVERVIEW   *Like Bacon and Hobbes, prose writers of the early 17th Century also turned away from the highly ornamental and artificial style of Lyly and Sidney, helping to fashion a new kind of precise English prose, elegant, but yet unadorned. The subject matter of prose greatly broadened, incorporating all phases of learning—even fishermen's lore—as the province of reflective prose.*

Robert Burton (1577–1640): A reclusive Oxford scholar, Burton wrote *The Anatomy of Melancholy* (1621–51), a book that grew with each succeeding edition until it reached nearly a half million words and included interesting observations on hundreds of subjects, gleaned from a lifetime of prodigious reading. Burton attempted to define melancholy as an emotional ailment (with special references to melancholia caused by love and religion) and to offer cures. He counteracted his own melancholy tendencies with a love of life and a sense of humor. *The Anatomy of Melancholy* has hundreds of allusions to literature—ancient and Elizabethan—and many authors used it as the source of their literary ideas.

Izaak Walton (1593–1683): His best-known work is *The Compleat Angler, or the Contemplative Man's Recreation,* the classic book about the lore of fish and fishing that evokes an England of pristine streams, inviting meadows, and cosy taverns. It takes the form of dialogues among the author Piscator (a fisherman), Auceps (a fowler), and Venator (a hunter), each commending his own sport. The author instructs his pupil in the art of catching various kinds of freshwater fish and dressing them for the table. An account of a fishing expedition along the river Lea also contains interludes of verse and song, angling anecdotes, moral reflections, and snatches of mythology and folklore.

John Selden (1584–1654): One of the first great critical scholars of modern England, he is now chiefly known for *Table Talk* (1689) a book of his sayings that were collected and edited by his secretary, Richard Milward. The book shows Selden to be a witty conversationalist with a mind capable of shrewd analysis. The subject matter deals with a wide range of human activities in a balanced, common sense way.

Sir Thomas Browne (1606–1682): Like Burton, this provincial physician loved the quaint and unusual.

- *Religio Medici* ("A Physician's Religion") was written from the point of view of an experimental scientist who has a wide interest in nature along with a rare charm and a sense of humor.
- *Hydriotaphia, Urn-Burial* begins with the discovery of some Roman funeral urns near Norwich and grows into a treatise on all known burial practices as well as an exhaustive investigation into death itself.

KEY QUOTATION

The Egyptians were afraid of fire, not as a deity but a devouring element mercilessly consuming their bodies and leaving too little of them; and therefore by precious embalmments. . . contrived the notablest ways of integral conservation.

—Hydriotaphia

- *The Garden of Cyrus* (1658), published in the same volume as *Urn Burial,* is an elaborate playing upon a conceit in prose. He uses the figure of the quincunx (the geometric arrangement of the five dots on dominoes or dice) to show the presence of the number five in art, astronomy, history, anatomy, magic, and nearly everything else.

The Character Writers: They wrote short sketches of various human "types."

- **Joseph Hall** (1574–1656), who claimed, with some validity, to be the first English satirist, wrote *Characters of Virtues and Vices* (1608), including short vignettes, written in a witty, homely style, about characters such as "The Malcontent."
- **Sir Thomas Overbury** (1581–1613) and some of his friends continued the genre in a book published in 1614 that, unlike Hall, included male and female characters with no arbitrary division between the good and the bad. Well-known sketches include "A Puritan" and "A Fair and Happy Milkmaid."
- **John Earle** (c.1601–1665) is considered the greatest of the character writers for his book *Microcosmography* ("The World in Little"), which describes, with humor and tolerance, "A Young Raw Preacher," "An Upstart Knight," and "A Pretender to Learning."

Key 24   The King James Bible

OVERVIEW   *This Authorized Version of the Bible, called the "noblest monument of English prose" was published in 1611 and had a profound influence on the phrasing, cadence, and vocabulary of both everyday speech and literature from the 17th century onward. It was the chief reading of the Puritans, who passed laws compelling the study and reading of it.*

Origin: King James summoned a conference in 1604 to discuss the revising of the Bible. He appointed 47 scholars, to be divided into six groups, instructing them to approach the revision conservatively.

The King James style: Much of the grand style of the Authorized Version comes from the work of two translators of the Bible into vernacular English: **William Tyndale** (c.1494–1536), who suffered a martyr's death for his translation of the New Testament, and **Miles Coverdale** (1488–1568), who translated the Old Testament. Both had the gift of placing simple words in musical cadences.

KEY QUOTATION

Every valley shall be exalted, and every mountain and hill shall be made low: and the crooked shall be made straight, and the rough places plain:
And the glory of the Lord shall be revealed, and all flesh shall see it together: for the mouth of the Lord hath spoken it.

—from *Isaiah*, 33:3

Influence on literature: The Victorian critic Matthew Arnold wrote of "one English book and one only, where . . . perfect plainness of speech is allied with perfect nobleness, and that book is the Bible." Scriptural phraseology has found its way into allusions and modified quotations (as in "selling a birthright" for a "mess of pottage") and into common speech ("highways and hedges," "thorn in the flesh," and "a soft answer turneth away wrath"). The King James Version of the Bible has not only supplied authors with spiritual themes, from Milton's *Paradise Lost* and Bunyan's *Pilgrim's Progress* to T.S. Eliot and W.H. Auden, but all had a major influence on innumerable writers in the cadence of its majestic prose.

Theme 4 RENAISSANCE POETRY

*T*he ability to write poetry was considered a necessary accomplishment for a Renaissance gentleman, and many courtiers were indeed accomplished poets. The sonnet form, introduced from Italy, was immediately popular and a number of sonnet cycles were produced. Lyrics, generally on the theme of love, were frequently pastoral and filled with imagery from nature. Religious themes are particularly important in the 17th century, a time of great religious conflict in England.

Key 25   Early Renaissance poets:
Wyatt and Surrey

OVERVIEW   *Typical of the Tudor poets were Sir Thomas Wyatt and Henry Howard, Earl of Surrey, aristocrats who wrote lyric poetry to be circulated among acquaintances.*

Foreign influences: Both Wyatt and Surrey translated and imitated classical Latin and Greek poems as well as contemporary French and Italian poets. They both used Italian verse forms *terza rima* and *ottava rima* and experimented with stanzaic forms, particularly the **sonnet**, adapting the Italian sonnet to an English variant with three quatrains and a couplet (called the Shakespearean sonnet).

The Renaissance Miscellanies: Many collections of poetry, called "Miscellanies," were published during the Tudor period. They contained primarily lyric poems, many of them free translations by various poets. The best-known was *Tottel's Miscellany* (1557), which contains 97 poems by Wyatt, 40 by Surrey.

Sir Thomas Wyatt (1503–1542): By age 25 he had served Henry VIII in missions to the Continent, where he became interested in love poetry, particularly by Petrarch.
- **Brings sonnet to England**: Influenced by Petrarchan sonnets, Wyatt began writing poems in English with the same form: fourteen lines, divided into eight- and six-line sections (**octaves** and **sestets**).
- **Subject matter**: Nearly all follow the traditions of **courtly love** and catalog the agonies inflicted by a cruel mistress on a love-sick knight. *Example:* "The Lover Compareth His State to a Ship in Perilous Storm Tossed on the Sea."

Henry Howard, Earl of Surrey (c.1517–1547): As a prominent aristocrat and a practicing poet, Surrey did much to establish the tradition of courtly concern with arts and letters.
- **Blank verse**: The first use of **blank verse** (unrhymed iambic pentameter) in English was in Surrey's translation of a part of the *Aeneid* in 1554.
- **Subject matter**: Surrey continued the Tudor tradition of sonnets about the pains and pangs of love. *Example:* "Description of Spring Wherein Each Thing Renews Save Only the Lover."

Key 26   Spenser and his works

OVERVIEW   *The poetry of Edmund Spenser (c.1552–1599), particularly* The Faerie Queene, *continues in the allegorical verse tradition of the Middle Ages. Spenser's allegories, however, were much more complex than previous ones.*

The Faerie Queene (Books I-III, 1590; Books IV-VI, 1596): Spenser's monumental scheme for this work is comparable in scope to Dante's *Divine Comedy*. Spenser hoped to present nothing less than the total civilization of his era. He planned first to portray eleven private moral virtues, each portrayed by a knightly figure, with Arthur summing up all virtues in the twelfth book. Next would come twelve more allegorical books, celebrating the political virtues of Arthur after he became king. Only six books were completed.

Allegory: Complexities come from the structure of the allegory on three levels: moral, historical, and personal. Allegories are suggested by the characters' names: Vanity, Queen of Pride, Gluttony. Readers should be alert to the multi-level meaning of each character. *Example:* The Red Cross Knight stands for the abstraction "holiness," for the English church, and, on a personal level, for the courtier Sir Philip Sidney.

Neoplatonism: The philosophy of Neoplatonism, which was widely held in the Renaissance, advocates finding permanence in the ever-changing world of nature by practicing the virtues, particularly love. Much allegorical meaning in the poem is based on Neoplatonism.

Stanzaic form: Spenser devised a nine-line stanza, rhyming *abab bcbcc*, now known as the Spenserian stanza. The first eight lines of the stanza are in iambic pentameter; the last is an **Alexandrine** (iambic hexameter).

Other works by Spenser:
- *The Shepherds Calender* (1579) includes twelve eclogues, one for each month, that lean heavily on classical pastoral poetry by Theocritus, which idealizes shepherds and rural life. An **eclogue** is a "singing match"; in these conventional poems, all shepherds are poets.
- *Amoretti* (1595) is a sonnet sequence celebrating the poet's courtship of Elizabeth Boyle.
- *The Epithalamion* (1595), called the most beautiful nuptial poem in any language, celebrates the poet's wedding to Miss Boyle.

Key 27 Other Elizabethan poets

OVERVIEW *An extraordinary period of creativity in po-etry occurred during the latter years of Elizabeth's reign and the early years of James I. There were aristocratic poets (called the "courtly lyricists") as well as students of more modest birth at Oxford and Cambridge (the "University Wits").*

Edward de Vere, 17th Earl of Oxford (1550–1604): Considered the best of the courtly poets for such sonnets as "Who Taught Thee First to Sigh?" or such lyrics as "If Women Could Be Fair," Oxford has been proposed to be the true author of plays attributed to Shakespeare.

Sir Edward Dyer (c.1550–1607): Highly popular in the royal court for a brief period, he is remembered for "My Mind to Me a Kingdom Is," asserting the Renaissance idea of intellectual self-sufficiency.

Nicholas Breton (c.1545–c.1626): Earliest of the University school of poets and one of the most popular Elizabethan pastoral lyricists, his "Phillida and Coridon," was written to be sung under the Queen's window.

Thomas Lodge (c.1558–1625): His *Rosalynde* (1590), a prose romance containing sonnets and eclogues, was the source of Shakespeare's *As You Like It*.

Samuel Daniel (c.1562–1619): Though the content of his verse lacked originality, he was noted for artistry with language, particularly in *Delia,* a sequence of fifty sonnets. He took English poetry a giant step forward with *The Complaint of Rosamund,* a monologue in **rime-royal** stanza.

Michael Drayton (1563–1631): A fashionable writer who produced all the types of verse popular in the Elizabethan age, Drayton is best known for his sonnet sequence *Ideas Mirrour* (1594) and *Idea, the Shepherd's Garland* (1593), a collection of pastoral eclogues.

Thomas Campion (1567–1620): An innovative versifier, Campion wrote four books of "Airs" (poems written to be sung) from 1601–c. 1617 that include some of the most perfect lyrics written in English, such as "When to Her Lute Corinna Sings" and "There is a Garden in Her Face."

Key 28   The Cavalier poets

OVERVIEW   *Called the "Tribe of Ben" because they were greatly influenced by Ben Jonson, they were sophisticated poets who supported the King and opposed the sober Puritans.*

Style: Their lyrics—indebted to the Latin poets Horace and Ovid—are characterized by symmetry of form, sensuousness, and a playful tone. Virtually ignoring the sonnet form, they excelled in lyrics characterized by short lines, idiomatic diction, and urbane wit.

Robert Herrick (1591–1674): The greatest of the Cavalier Poets, and the only one not a courtier, this rural vicar extolled the idea of *carpe diem* (seize the day, live vigorously) and wrote many joyous love poems. The best-known is "To the Virgins to Make Much of Time," with the opening: "Gather ye rosebuds while ye may, old time is still a-flying." His poems also show an interest in the ancient folk festivals of rural England like May Day and Harvest Home, as in, "Corinna's Going A-Maying." Some of his best lyrics are highly polished exercises in miniature, such as "Upon Julia's Clothes."

Thomas Carew (c.1595–1639): He wrote lyric poems with a classical polish learned from Jonson. His primary subject was delicate seduction, but form, rhythms, and structure interested him more than content. He was appreciated for his graceful and sometimes cynical songs, such as "Ask Me No More Where Jove Bestows."

Sir John Suckling (1609–1642): His greatest contribution to poetry was to use the language of ordinary conversation among courtiers. He used irony and realism in dealing with conventional love themes, as in "Why So Pale and Wan, Fair Lover?"

Richard Lovelace (1618–1658): He was the versatile Renaissance man who wrote acceptably all the standard forms of amorous verse, e.g., the song beginning "Lucasta frown and let me die, But smile and let me live." Better known is the idealist lyric "To Lucasta, Going to the Wars," which asserts: "I could not love thee (Deare) so much, Lov'd I not Honour more."

Key 29   John Donne and metaphysical
poetry

OVERVIEW   *"Metaphysical poetry" synthesizes passion and intellect, to display both feeling and learning.*

Imagery: Religion and romantic love are the two principal subjects, but the startling imagery and the far-reaching allusions to philosophy, geography, and astronomy give complexity to themes that were quite simple to the Cavalier Poets.

John Donne (1572–1631): He made a strong break with the flowery poetry of the Elizabethans and the Cavaliers. He read widely in science, theology, and nearly all the branches of learning, and he had the lively imagination and boldness to use unusual imagery in traditional situations: rotting corpses appear in love poems alongside compasses and astronomical data. Though unwilling, Donne became an outstanding preacher in an age of great preachers. His religious poems, full of paradoxes and ambiguities, are among the greatest.

Donne's poetry: In addition to startling imagery, Donne frequently relies on conversational language and tone to give the lyrics a sense of immediacy. His poems deal with both secular and religious themes.

- **"Go and Catch a Falling Star"** wittily comments on the impossibility of finding a faithful woman.
- **"The Indifferent"** is spoken by a bachelor who demands "inconstancy" in love.
- **"A Valediction Forbidding Mourning"** is a love poem written as Donne embarks on a journey. He uses the metaphor of a compass (of the type used in drawing a circle) to show the union of the two lovers even as they are separated.
- **"The Flea"** is a clever seduction poem suggesting an unlikely vehicle for the physical union of the blood of two lovers: the stomach of a flea.
- **"The Ecstasy"** makes a mystical religious experience of the joining of the souls of two lovers.
- **"The Canonization"** is a philosophical love poem.
- **"Good Friday, 1613. Riding Westward"** has the poet turn his back to the scene of the Crucifixion to receive "corrections."

- *Holy Sonnets,* including "Death Be Not Proud" and "Batter My Heart, Three-Personned God" are powerful evocations of the Divine. "The Litany" is a rhapsodic lyric about the eternal power of the Church.

KEY QUOTATION:

Our two souls therefore, which are one,
Though I must go, endure not yet
A breach, but an expansion,
Like gold to airy thinness beat.

If they be two, they are two so
As stiff twin compasses are two;
Thy soul, the fixt foot, makes no show
To move, but doth, if th'other do.

        —from "A Valediction: Forbidding Mourning"

George Herbert (1593–1633): He uses simpler, more traditional imagery in religious poetry than Donne. He demonstrates a deep religious faith in **"Virtue"** (contrasting the transitory world with eternal spiritual existence) and **"The Collar"** (which turns a symbol of slavery into one of submissiveness to God). *The Temple*, containing nearly all of his surviving poems, was published in 1633. The Romantic Age revived interest in Herbert's poems, largely due to praise by Coleridge.

Richard Crashaw (c.1613–1649): The son of a militant Puritan clergyman, Crashaw rebelled and became a Roman Catholic. He unifies the sensual and the spiritual in traditional Church imagery in such poems as **"The Flaming Heart,"** extolling the Spanish nun, St. Theresa. His principal work was *Steps to the Temple* (1646), a collection of religious poems influenced by Spanish mystics.

Henry Vaughan (1621–1695): Inspired by Herbert, but less traditional, Vaughan uses Neoplatonic mysticism to reach the heights of religious ecstasy. His best-known poem is **"The Retreat,"** which depicts childhood as a period of divine spirituality (and points forward to Wordsworth's "Immortality Ode," Key 56). In it, he writes of his own "Angel-infancy," when he would muse on clouds and flowers and see in them "some shadows of eternity."

Key 30 John Milton and his works

OVERVIEW *John Milton (1608–1674), the most continuously admired English author except for Shakespeare, stood in time between the Renaissance and the Commonwealth. His writings combine the restless intellectual spirit of the earlier period with the later emphasis on religion and politics.*

Religious themes: Unlike Donne's, Milton's religious poetry is unrelated to ordinary life; the visions he saw in his blindness were of Heaven or Hell, archangels or demons.

Early poems: Best-known are the brief companion pieces (c. 1631): **"L'Allegro"** (describing the "cheerful" man) and **"Il Penseroso"** (the "studious, contemplative" man). **"Lycidas"** (1637) is a **pastoral elegy** on the death of his friend, the poet Edward King.

Prose (1640-1660): His most important tract was *Areopagitica* (1644), a strong argument against censorship. *Of Education* (1644) advocates the kind of education that produces versatile, scholarly gentlemen.

Paradise Lost: This is Milton's monumental epic poem in twelve books of superb blank verse. Based on the Bible and other writings available in the Renaissance, the epic begins with the fall from Heaven of the rebel angels, and continues through Satan's temptation of Adam and Eve and their expulsion from the Garden of Eden. Though some have argued that Satan is the epic hero, the real hero is mankind, and the dramatic conflict is within humanity's divided propensity for good and evil.

Sonnets: The 23 sonnets of Milton are ranked second only to the sonnets of Shakespeare in excellence. Among the best are **"When I Consider How My Light is Spent"** (about serving God, though blind), and **"How Soon Hath Time"** (the realization at age 24 of time's quick passage).

Later long works: *Paradise Regained* (1671), which depicts Christ's temptations, has little of the baroque splendor of *Paradise Lost. Samson Agonistes* (1671) is like a Greek tragedy in its treatment of Samson's downfall.

Key 31 Other Commonwealth poets

OVERVIEW *During the era of the Commonwealth, or "Free State" (1649–1660), under Oliver Cromwell, even poets were divided into opposing political camps: the pro-Commonwealth "parliamentarians" and the pro-monarchy "royalists."*

Poets: Except for Milton, the only great parliamentarian poet was Marvell. The two best royalist poets, Cowley and Waller, wrote lyrics that are closer to the style of Dryden and Pope (Keys 42 and 49) in the Neoclassical Period ahead than to the style of Donne and Milton.

Andrew Marvell (1621–1678): The unofficial laureate to Oliver Cromwell, he mourned Cromwell's death in "Upon the Death of His Late Highness the Lord Protector" in 1658 and took part in the funeral procession. His few poems were remarkably diverse in style and of a high quality. **"To His Coy Mistress"** (1681) is a *carpe diem* poem that wittily suggests that with unlimited time he could catalogue his mistress's charms, but since time is short, "seizing the day" and tasting immediate pleasures is imperative. He was neglected for two centuries, and it was not until after World War II, with the publication of T.S. Eliot's essay "Andrew Marvell," that his modern high reputation was secured. His forte was treating conventional themes with such originality and wit that they seemed new.

Abraham Cowley (1618–1667): A precocious poet, he wrote his first poem at ten and a successful volume of verse at fifteen. At his death his reputation was lofty, primarily for *The Mistress* (1647), a sequence of love poems that included the popular lyric **"The Wish,"** a pretty eulogy of country life. He was also praised for his **"Pindarique odes,"** in which he introduced the type of irregular ode much imitated by John Dryden (Key 42) and others.

Edmund Waller (1606–1687): Though writing later in the Restoration Period, Waller was strongly influenced by Jonson and wrote in the Cavalier tradition. He wrote in easy, conversational language in his famous lyric, **"Go, Lovely Rose"** and the witty **"On a Girdle."** John Dryden praised his "sweetness," calling him "the father of English numbers" (*numbers* being another word for *meter*).

Theme 5 RENAISSANCE DRAMA

*T*he figure of Shakespeare towers above all other English authors, of both the Renaissance and all other periods. Drama at this time has moved completely into the secular world. Blank verse becomes the standard form for drama, except for scenes of "low" comedy, which are in prose. Many early plays were based on the Latin comedies of Plautus and Terence and the tragedies of Seneca. The revenge tragedy is a popular form, reaching its apotheosis in Shakespeare's *Hamlet*. The fact that female roles are played by young boys makes somewhat more plausible the standard plot device of the girl disguised as a boy in romantic comedies.

Key 32 Pre-Shakespearean drama

OVERVIEW   *Miracle plays and morality plays continued to be performed through most of the 16th century, along with secular plays, called "interludes" and two other specialized genres: academic drama (performed in schools by student actors) and drama of the court (produced in holiday seasons for the Queen). Public theater began in 1576, when the first permanent theater for public performances was built in a London suburb under the leadership of James Burbage.*

Interludes: Although didactic, like the morality plays, these were more comic and realistic, and the heroes more individualized.
  - **Henry Medwall** (fl. 1490): His interlude *Fulgens and Lucres* (c.1497) is probably the first purely secular drama in English. It was written for presentation between the courses of a banquet.
  - **John Heywood** (c.1497–c.1580): The best-known interlude is Heywood's short comedy, *The Play Called the Foure PP: A Newe and Very Merry Interlude of A Palmer, A Pardoner, A Pothycary, A Pedlar* (c.1523). In a match to determine the most fantastic lie, the Palmer wins by saying he had never in all his travels seen a woman lose her temper.

Academic comedy: Nicholas Udall's *Ralph Roister Doister* (c.1535) is modeled on the Latin comedies of Plautus and Terence; the hero is Ralph, a penniless braggart of a soldier. The anonymous *Gammer Gurton's Needle* (c.1553) is more humorous; the simple plot has the whole community involved in retrieving Gammer's lost needle.

Academic tragedy: The Roman tragic dramatist Seneca was the model for the tragedies performed in Elizabethan schools. *Gorboduc, or Ferrex and Porrex* (1561–62) by two lawyers, Thomas Sackville and Thomas Norton, is termed the first true English tragedy. Gorboduc divides his kingdom between his sons, leading to a quarrel and one brother's slaying the other. Blank verse is used for the first time in drama.

Court drama: By royal decree dramas and other entertainments were performed at court on festival days such as Christmas and Twelfth Night. One source of drama was the law schools, and from one of these, Gray's Inn, came the comedy *Supposes*, by George Gascoigne, the earliest comedy in English prose. It is filled with Euphuistic puns and other figures of speech. Richard Edwards wrote many court dramas, among them *Damon and Pithias* (pub. 1571). John Lyly, the author of *Euphues* (Key 21), also wrote six plays for the choirboys of the Chapel Royal.

Drama in the public theater: A number of characteristic Renaissance themes, characters, and plot devices were introduced:

- John Lyly's *Galathea* (c.1588) is the first English use of the device of **girls disguised as boys**, used many times by Shakespeare.
- George Peele's *The Old Wives Tale* (c.1590) is a dramatic fairy tale that initiates Elizabethan **romantic comedy**.
- Robert Greene's *The Honorable History of Friar Bacon and Friar Bungay* (1594) is a romantic comedy notable for the virtuous and charming heroine Margaret, the first of her type on the English stage.
- Thomas Kyd's *The Spanish Tragedy* (c.1586), the most popular play before 1600, was the first English **"revenge tragedy,"** outdoing Seneca in violent horror. Kyd made original use of feigned madness and a play-within-a-play.

KEY QUOTATION

In time the savage bull sustains the yoke,
In time all haggard hawks will stoop to lure,
In time small wedges cleave the hardest oak,
In time the flint is pierced with softest shaver.

—*The Spanish Tragedy* I. Vl.3

Violence: Extremely popular in the new professional theater, violent action often left the stage strewn with corpses.

- John Pickeryng's *A Newe Enterlude of Vice Conteyninge the Historye of Horestes (pub. 1567),* which roughly relates the classical tale of Orestes and uses a character, Vice, from the morality plays, has much gratuitous violence, with the stage littered with bloody corpses.
- Thomas Preston's *A Lamentable Tragedie, Mixed Full of Plesant Mirth, Containing the Life of Cambises, King of Percia (c.1569)* has six men and two boys handling 38 roles. Blood covers the floor of the stage as a fake skin is flayed from an attempted usurper, and a bladder of wine is nicked to simulate the flowing of his life's blood. There is much **low comedy** (the "plesant mirth" of the title) and ranting in the **bombastic** style of the day.

Key 33   Shakespeare

OVERVIEW   *There are very few clearly established facts about the life of England's greatest dramatist and poet, **William Shakespeare** (1564–1616).*

Biography: After his marriage to Anne Hathaway and the birth of twins, Shakespeare left his native Stratford for London about 1587. First a minor actor, he began writing plays. Robert Greene (*Groatsworth of Wit*, 1592) spoke of him as "an upstart crow, beautiful with our feathers, that with his tiger's heart wrapped in a player's hide, supposes he is as well able to bombast out a blank verse as the best of you." His first published work was a poem, **Venus and Adonis** (1593); his first published drama, *Titus Andronicus*, appeared anonymously a year later. He wrote 37 plays before retiring to Stratford, where he died April 23, 1616.

Career as a poet: During the 1590s, Shakespeare wrote sonnets that were published as a sequence in 1609 and are considered his finest work except for the dramas. His sonnet sequence follows the lead of Sidney and Spenser, but eclipses them in poetic quality and originality. Motifs in the sonnets include: the beauty of a young man and the poet's involvement with him, a "dark lady," a rival poet, and the ravages of time and the immortality of art.

Authorship disputed: Shakespeare was accepted as the author of the plays until 1769, when Herbert Lawrence argued that a relatively uneducated minor actor could not have produced the Shakespearean canon. Theorists have proposed Sir Francis Bacon, Christopher Marlowe, or the Earl of Oxford, as the true author of the plays. There is no evidence to support these conjectures.

Texts: All printed plays by Shakespeare appeared in small cheap quartos until 1623, when the first of four folio editions was published. It contained 36 plays, divided arbitrarily into histories, comedies, and tragedies. The third folio, though not the others, includes *Pericles*.

KEY QUOTATION

That time of year thou mayst in me behold
When yellow leaves, or none, or few, do hang
Upon those boughs which shake against the cold,
Bare ruined choirs, where late the sweet birds sang.

—from "Sonnet 73"

Key 34 Shakespeare's history plays

OVERVIEW *The history plays cover the reigns of earlier English kings, and frequently deal with the nature of kingship and the qualities of a "good" king. These so-called chronicle plays—an Elizabethan invention—served as Shakespeare's apprenticeship to the drama.*

Minor plays: *Henry VI, parts I, II, and III* (c.1590–92) and *The Life and Death of King John* (c.1595–96) are melodramatic accounts of royal power struggles during chaotic periods of English history.

The Tragedy of King Richard III (c.1592): Called a chronicle play as well as a "Fall of Princes" tragedy, it depicts the hunch-backed Richard's violent route to the throne, succeeding Edward IV. One of Shakespeare's earliest well-developed characters, Richard is pure villain, murdering all who stand in his way.

KEY QUOTATION

My conscience has a thousand several tongues,
And every tongue brings in a several tale,
And every tale condemns me for a villain.

—from *Richard III*

The Tragedy of Richard II (c.1597): It relates the conflict between the popular Henry Bolingbroke and the eloquent but weak and inept Richard II, whose real opponent is himself. Only as he is being assassinated does Richard finally take direct action.

The First Part of Henry IV (c.1597): Shakespeare combines the comedy of the amoral, drunken, but joyous Falstaff with the exploits of the wild young Prince Hal, son of Henry IV. In the course of the play, Hal slays Hotspur, but he lets Falstaff pretend to be the hero.

The Second Part of Henry IV (c.1598): Continuing Part One, Shakespeare allows the comedy of Falstaff to dominate a play somewhat barren in historical events. When Henry IV dies, Hal, now Henry V, sternly dismisses Falstaff and turns to the business of kingship.

The Life of Henry V (1599): This patriotic play depicts Henry's triumphs in France and also portrays him as an ideal ruler, possessed of the Platonic virtues of justice, fortitude, temperance, and wisdom.

Key 35   Shakespeare's comedies and
romances

OVERVIEW   *The comedies varied widely in type, including masque fantasies, romantic comedy, farces, and problem comedies. His last plays are more nearly dramatic romances than strict comedies.*

The Comedy of Errors (c.1590–93): A farce about the mistaken identities occurring among twin men with twin slaves. Based heavily on Plautus, Shakespeare molds it toward romantic comedy.

The Two Gentlemen of Verona (c.1590–94): Thin in plot, the play blends low comedy with poetic passages in blank verse. The favorite plot of the disguised girl pursuing her lover is first used here.

Love's Labour's Lost (c.1590–94): This satire on utopian concepts has four noblemen vow to study for three years, avoiding all contact with women. The Princess of France and her beautiful attendants soon foil the plan. Notable are the characters Biron—the first of Shakespeare's intellectual heroes—and Rosaline, a witty heroine.

A Midsummer's Night's Dream (c.1591–96): This masque fantasy is best known for the mischievous elfin character Puck and the comic artisan Bottom, who, with his fellow tradesmen, put on a ludicrous play.

The Taming of the Shrew (c.1594–97): A farce in which the clever Petruchio woos the shrewish and mean-tempered Katharina, weds her for her dowry, and curbs her will.

The Merchant of Venice (c.1596–97): The love affair between Bassanio and Portia, is complicated by a loan from Shylock, who demands his money or a pound of flesh. Portia, disguised as a lawyer, solves the dilemma.

The Merry Wives of Windsor (c.1598–1600): It was written for Queen Elizabeth, who requested a Falstaff comedy. Falstaff sends identical love letters to merry wives who conspire with their husbands to humble him in a comic way.

Much Ado About Nothing (c.1598–1600): This romantic comedy features the witty repartee of two unlikely lovers: Benedick and Beatrice, both determined to remain single.

As You Like It (1599–1600): In this romantic pastoral comedy, court intrigue contrasts with country life. Touchstone is the first of Shakespeare's "wise fools."

Twelfth Night, or What You Will (1600–01): Again a woman (Viola) is dressed as a man in this romantic comedy of intricate plot. There are two memorable comic characters: Sir Toby Belch and Sir Andrew Aguecheek.

All's Well That Ends Well (c.1603): After *Twelfth Night* the comedies grew darker in tone. Helena saves the life of King Bertram and demands him as her husband. She deceives him into fathering her child.

Measure for Measure (c.1604): This problem comedy has Angelo offer to save the life of the condemned Claudio in exchange for sexual favors from his sister Isabella, a novice in a nunnery. She refuses, but through disguises and subterfuges, the matter is solved.

Troilus and Cressida (c.1598–1602): This play is so enigmatic that scholars debate whether to call it a comedy or a tragedy. Set during the Trojan War, the action is tragic, but its cynicism and satire suggest a comedy.

Pericles, Prince of Tyre (c.1608): This dark comedy is based on the premise that Thaisa, wife of Pericles, is mistakenly thought to have died in childbirth and is buried at sea.

Cymbeline (1609–10): In a tragi-comedy somewhat like *Othello,* the pure Imogen is falsely accused of infidelity by the Iago-like Iachimo. Though ordered killed, she escapes in a page-boy disguise. All are reunited in an elaborate recognition scene at the end.

The Winter's Tale (c.1610–11): In this dramatic romance, King Leontes falsely believes his wife Hermione has taken his friend Polixenes as a lover and tries to poison him. While Hermione is mistakenly imprisoned for the deed, she bears a child. Much later, with the help of the oracle at Delphi, all are reunited happily.

The Tempest (c.1611): In his last play, Shakespeare bids his farewell to the theater. Symbolically, Prospero, the magician in the play, renounces magic and returns to the real world. Memorable characters are Ariel, a spiritual creature, and Caliban (an acronym for "cannibal") who represents the baser side of human nature.

Key 36   Shakespeare's tragedies

OVERVIEW   *The almost unearthly power and richness of Shakespeare's mind is most evident in his crowning achievement, the four great tragedies of* Hamlet, Othello, King Lear, *and* Macbeth. *He also wrote six other plays that can be categorized as tragedies, as well as several history plays with subject matter relating to the downfall of a monarch (called "Fall of Princes" tragedies).*

Early tragedies: The four tragedies dated before 1603, written at intervals from each other, differ markedly in style and tone. All four can be related to the revenge plays of Seneca.
- *The Tragedy of Titus Andronicus* (c.1592–94): In this revenge tragedy, Titus, a roman general, captures Queen Tamora and her sons. He sacrifices one son, and Tamora's awful revenge culminates in a dinner of human flesh.
- *The Tragedy of Romeo and Juliet* (c.1595): Shakespeare's first romantic tragedy stems from a vendetta between the houses of Montague and Capulet, leading to the deaths of the two "star-crossed" lovers. The play begins with a sonnet spoken by the chorus, and in its poetic language it reflects the great interest in sonnets in the 1590s.
- *The Tragedy of Julius Caesar* (c.1598–1601): This popular "Fall of Princes" tragedy is also a Senecan tragedy with a revenge motif. It is unusual in structure: Julius Caesar dies in Act II, and Brutus does not emerge as the dominant character until the last half of the play.
- *The Tragedy of Hamlet, Prince of Denmark* (c.1601): This tragedy of the revenge of a prince for the murder of his father goes far beyond Seneca in its philosophical complexity and is considered the greatest work of English literary art. The glorious poetry and the multi-layered characterization makes the title role, as Samuel Pepys wrote, "the best part, I believe, that ever was acted."

Middle tragedies: The great triad of tragedies that Shakespeare wrote from c.1604–06 are similar in depicting a world full of inscrutable and interesting evil, presented objectively, not broodingly and subjectively (as in *Hamlet*).
- *The Tragedy of Othello, Moor of Venice* (c.1604): One of the most poetic and best-constructed of the tragedies, *Othello* has three memorable characters—the heroic Othello, the villainous

Iago, and the pure and loving Desdemona—whose interaction, engendered by the envious Iago, leads to terrible consequences. Coleridge, in a memorable phrase, describes Iago's soliloquy at the end of Act I, scene 3 as "the motive hunting of motiveless malignity."

- *The Tragedy of King Lear* (c.1605–6): This is a tragedy of the fall of an aging king—a petulant and unwise old man—who divides his kingdom among three daughters. Two malicious daughters persuade him to disinherit the sincere Cordelia, leading to the tragic ending of Lear's madness, Cordelia's being hanged, and the recovered Lear dying of grief.
- *The Tragedy of Macbeth* (c.1606): The cruel, overpowering ambition of Macbeth and Lady Macbeth motivates a tragedy that is Shakespeare's most vivid picture of raw, naked evil. The prophecy of the witches begins the play, and Macbeth's attempts to thwart his destiny and defeat the witches' warning motivates much tragedy.

KEY QUOTATION

Methought I heard a voice cry, 'Sleep no more!
Macbeth doth murder sleep,' the innocent sleep
Sleep that knits up the ravelled sleave of care,
The death of each day's life, sore labour's bath,
Balm of hurt minds, great nature's second course,
Chief nourisher of life's feast.

—Macbeth

Later tragedies: The last three tragedies do not approach the greatness of the previously written ones, and only one, *Antony and Cleopatra*, is frequently performed.

- *Antony and Cleopatra* (c.1607): The tragic love affair between the noble hero Antony and Queen Cleopatra destroys Antony, but transforms Cleopatra from a selfish, wanton girl to a true queen who dies triumphantly.
- *The Life of Timon of Athens* (c.1605–08): Though published in the First Folio, this tragedy of the fall of Timon seems incomplete.
- *The Tragedy of Coriolanus* (c.1606–08): Honored with the surname Coriolanus for capturing the town Corioli, this Roman general shows contempt for the mob, leading to his banishment from Rome. He leads an army against Rome, causing a tragic dilemma as he attacks his own family.

Key 37 Other Elizabethan and Jacobean dramatists

OVERVIEW *The Elizabethan Age had many extraordinary playwrights, but the only two who came close to rivalling Shakespeare were Christopher Marlowe, who made blank verse an instrument of eloquence and grandeur in his tragedies, and Ben Jonson, the master of classical, satirical comedy.*

Christopher Marlowe (1564–93): Marlowe's robust, poetic plays each dealt with the consuming desire of one overwhelming figure. He had a strong sense of the theater, moving his audiences with startling stage maneuvers.

- *Tamburlaine the Great* (Part I, c.1587; Part II, c.1588): Tamburlaine, a ruthless shepherd-robber, plots his bloody route to the throne of Persia. In Part II his gory conquests continue as he ravages Egypt and Babylon. While Spenser was writing of virtuous Christian knights, Marlowe presented the consummate Renaissance egoist and villain. In one scene Tamburlaine imprisons the Turkish emperor and his empress in a cage, goading them with cruel taunts until they dash out their brains against the bars of the cage.

- *The Tragical History of Dr. Faustus* (c.1589): The German scholar Faustus, bored with conventional learning, sells his soul to the Devil for superhuman powers. He misuses his powers by playing tricks on the Pope and calling up Helen of Troy, with the well-known line: "Was this the face that launched a thousand ships. . ." At the end, though Faustus is repentant, Lucifer claims his soul. The anguish in Faustus's mind is poignantly depicted.

- *The Jew of Malta* (c.1591): Barabas has half his wealth confiscated by the Governor of Malta, and his plot for revenge begins an orgy of slaughter in which his daughter Abigail's lover is killed and Abigail herself is poisoned. At the end Barabas dies by falling into a boiling caldron.

- *The Troublesome Reign and Lamentable Death of Edward the Second* (c.1592): A weak English king is involved in political intrigue and assassinated in this "Fall of Princes" tragedy.

Ben Jonson (1572–1637): Jonson's chief contribution to drama was to enrich the possibilities of the genre called "comedy of humours," in which stock characters—cheeky slaves, miserly oldsters, and braggart soldiers—are played against each other. "Humours," are defined as "obsessive quirks of disposition."

- *Every Man in His Humours* (1598): Stock characters—a jealous husband, country bumpkin, deceived father, and simple squire—are linked together in an inconsequential plot, allowing Jonson to display the foibles of contemporary London life. Asper represents Jonson in the play and explains the playwright's theory of humors.

- *Volpone, or The Fox* (c.1605–06): Volpone, a rich Venetian, pretends to be fatally ill in order to receive gifts from his covetous acquaintances. Considered the greatest satiric comedy in English, it uses stock characters to expose greed. A secondary plot involves Sir Politic Would-be, an English traveller who has absurd schemes for improving trade and curing diseases.

- *The Alchemist* (1610): The character Subtle claims to be an alchemist who can change base metal to gold, thus entrapping the greedy, including a Puritan pastor.

George Chapman (c.1559–1634): His comic masterpiece, *All Fools* (c.1599–1604), combines two comedies by Terence into one comedy of intrigue.

John Marston (c.1565–1634): *The Malcontent* (1604) is a revenge tragedy replete with horror.

Thomas Dekker (c.1570–c.1632): He wrote one of the best-loved English comedies, *The Shoemaker's Holiday* (1599), with action placed realistically in Elizabethan London.

Thomas Heywood (c.1575–1641): He wrote the period's best domestic tragedy, *A Woman Killed with Kindness* (c.1603), successful despite its sentimental subplot.

John Webster (c.1580–c.1625): He wrote such sensational tragedies as *The White Devil, or Vittoria Corombona* (c.1607–12)—based on a real-life murder story—and *The Duchess of Malfi* (c.1612–14), also historical. Webster pioneered in making women central figures in his plays.

Theme 6 THE RESTORATION AND
THE 18TH CENTURY

When Charles II was restored to the English throne in 1660, he ruled a nation weary of revolution and civil war, eager to enjoy the worldly pleasures denied them by the somber Puritans. In 1665, the plague ravaged Britain, and the following year a fire destroyed most of London, and both events were thought to be the vengeance of Divine Providence. A series of wars against the French between 1689 and 1763 brought Britain the huge domains of Canada and India, but shortly afterwards, she lost her thirteen American colonies. In such a volatile age, great fortunes were amassed as poverty multiplied. The 18th century was a great age of advance in the physical sciences, with most discoveries being taken as proof of divine law and order. In literature there was a great emphasis on order and rules, particularly rules proposed by Aristotle, and correctness became more important than using creative imagination.

INDIVIDUAL KEYS IN THIS THEME

Key 38   Cultural characteristics

OVERVIEW   *When Charles Stuart returned from exile in France to become Charles II in 1660, he led the strong reaction to the drab Puritan way of life by reopening the theaters and heading a notoriously pleasure-loving court. The 18th century was an age of transition, marked by the beginning of the Industrial Revolution and the emergence of the British Empire.*

Intellectual life: Intellectual accomplishments by philosophers like John Locke and the mathematician Sir Isaac Newton led to a new respect for order and reason, fostering the love of conventional rules that gave the 18th century the name Neoclassical Period.

Literary conventionality: The Renaissance had revered Aristotle, and his *Poetics* had set the literary standards. In the Neoclassical period, Aristotle's concepts, such as the unities of time, place, and action in drama, became the fixed norm. Even some of Shakespeare's dramas were devalued because they did not observe these unities. On the positive side, the influence of the classical tradition led to a love of moderation, balance, and grace, coupled with a respect for intelligence and dignity.

Society: Although great wealth and rational order existed among the aristocracy, London's poor, as depicted in Hogarth's painting "Gin Lane," lived in miserable poverty at the mercy of a severe penal code that assigned the death penalty for stealing a handkerchief or murder. During most of the period, Dissenters (Protestants who opposed the Church of England) and Roman Catholics were excluded from public office.

The Literary scene: Though the first half of the 18th century was an age of great practicality and common sense, and reason and rationality were the hallmarks of Alexander Pope's unemotional, philosophical poems in couplets, the latter half of the century saw the rise of highly emotional, melancholy poets referred to as the "Graveyard School," precursors of the Romantic Age. It was also an age of great satire in prose and poetry. Though there was an elitist air of intellectualism in the works of Dryden and Pope, the 18th century was also the period in which popular literature, especially the novel, flourished.

Key 39 John Bunyan, popular allegorist

OVERVIEW *John Bunyan (1628–1688), one of the most remarkable figures of the 17th century, wrote the most successful allegory in English literature:* Pilgrim's Progress.

Popularity: The popularity of this book has been second only to the Bible. It was a universally read classic in England as well as Puritan New England and has been translated into nearly every language.

Early works: Beginning with his first publication, the controversial tract *Some Gospel Truths Opened* (1656), Bunyan was under attack. The Restoration was unkind to Nonconformists, and in 1661 Bunyan was imprisoned for twelve years; there he wrote *The Holy City* (1665); his spiritual autobiography, *Grace Abounding to the Chief of Sinners* (1666), and *A Confession of My Faith and a Reason of My Practice* (1672).

The Pilgrim's Progress from This World to That Which Is to Come: Written during a second imprisonment of six months in 1675, this is an allegory of the journey through life of Christian, the principal character.

Content: Christian meets many symbolic, but familiar objects along the way: a quagmire, the bypaths through pleasant meadows, the steep hill, Vanity Fair, the Slough of Despond. A superb story teller, Bunyan keeps his reader in suspense while teaching a moral lesson with his holy parables.

Style: He uses concrete language and vividly observed details in a style similar to the prose of the King James Bible (Key 24).

Status as literature: Bunyan's allegory was much admired by Swift, Johnson, and Cowper, but it was not considered great literature until the 1830s. *Pilgrim's Progress* is now considered the culmination of medieval allegory in the uncultured mind just as *The Faerie Queene* was its culmination among the educated.

KEY QUOTATION:

"As I walked through the wilderness of this world, I lighted on a certain place where was a Den, and I laid me down in that place to sleep; and, as I slept, I dreamed a dream."

Key 40   Restoration comedy

OVERVIEW   *In 1660, when the monarchy was restored and the London theaters were reopened after 24 years of silence imposed by the Puritan Parliament, people were starved for merriment of all kinds, particularly drama. Young Charles II, who had enjoyed plays during his exile in France, led the clamor. Playwrights obliged with a new type of play: the comedy of manners.*

Subject matter: The comedies of manners hold the mirror up to an artificial society motivated chiefly by a desire for pleasure. They satirize those who try to enter the fashionable charmed circle.

Style: These comedies rely on verbal fencing and repartee. The predominant tone is witty, bawdy, cynical, and amoral. The plays were written mainly in prose, with passages of verse being reserved for the most romantic moments.

Characters: The principal characters are fashionable people who place wit and the knowledge of what is ''good form'' above morality and ethics. Standard comic characters who attempt the social climb are dull-witted citizens, rural types, lawyers, and stock comic figures like misers, hypocrites, and aging, love-starved women. A favorite character is the **fop** who tries to imitate the grand manners of the genuine gallant.

KEY AUTHORS

Sir George Etherege (1635?–1691), in *The Man of Mode, or Sir Fopling Flutter* (1676) introduced the oft-imitated fop whose mannerisms make him easy prey to a man of wit and elegance.

William Wycherley (1641?–1715) presented vice scornfully in his somewhat indecent farce, *The Country Wife* (1675).

William Congreve (1670–1729) was the supreme master of witty dialogue. His *The Double Dealer* (1693), *Love for Love* (1695), and *The Way of the World* (1700) set high standards for his treatment of the familiar characters.

Sir John Vanbrugh (1664–1726) in his rowdy farce, *The Provoked Wife* (1697) created popular Sir John Brute.

George Farquhar (c.1677–1707) moved his plots outside narrow London society in his less-cynical plays: *The Recruiting Officer* (1706) and *The Beaux' Stratagem* (1707).

Key 41 Other Restoration dramas

OVERVIEW *Two types of serious plays dominated the Restoration stage: the heroic play and the Restoration tragedy.*

Heroic plays: The chief aim was to celebrate, on a grand scale, the subjects John Dryden defined for the genre: "love and valor." Later periods condemned these plays for the ridiculously bombastic dialogue, the rhymed heroic couplets, the stylized characters, and the overly complicated plots.
- John Dryden's *The Indian Queen* (1664), about Montezuma's forces defeating the Mexicans, was the first successful heroic play. Dryden (1631–1700) later wrote the elaborate *The Conquest of Granada,* in two parts (1670, 1671).
- The excesses of the heroic plays were burlesqued in 1671 by George Villier's comedy *The Rehearsal,* and the genre was never again popular.

Restoration tragedy: Improving on the heroic plays were the Restoration tragedies, which were more realistic in style, more naturally poetic in the blank verse meter, and more integrated in plot because they followed the dramatic unities of time, place, and action.
- Dryden's *All for Love* (1678), a version of the Antony and Cleopatra story, is the best-known of this genre. It concentrates on the last hours in the lives of the royal pair, and it is esteemed for its elaborately formal presentation of character, action, and theme.
- Thomas Otway (1652–1685) moved toward sentimental **pathos** in his tragedies, treating his exalted personages as if they were ordinary humans, speaking the natural language of the heart. *Venice Preserved* (1682) is his finest work, adding topical politics and some indecent comic scenes to passages of great pathos.
- Thomas Southerne (1660–1746) was an Irish dramatist whose *Fatal Marriage* (1694) and *Oroonoko* (1695) brought a new element to Restoration tragedy: an independent comic plot sandwiched into a serious story.

Key 42   Dryden and his works

OVERVIEW   *John Dryden (1631–1700) was by far the greatest literary figure in England at the end of the 17th century. He wrote heroic plays and tragedies (see Key 41), literary criticism, satiric poetry, and occasional poems (written to commemorate important events).*

Style: He sharpened the heroic couplet into a sophisticated poetic instrument and was innovative in adding conversational rhythms to prose and poetry. T.S. Eliot wrote that Dryden "found the English speechless and he gave them speech."

Literary criticism: His masterpiece, *Essay of Dramatic Poesy* (1665) defends English drama against the French, which he believed was "too strictly tied up" with Neoclassical rules. He objected to the triteness and faulty morals of the plots taken from Roman plays and defended the use of rhymed verse in plays.

Satire: *Absalom and Achitophel* (written in heroic couplets) attacks those who supported Charles's illegitimate son, the Duke of Monmouth, to succeed him. *The Medal* (1682) is satire directed at the Earl of Shaftesbury, acquitted of charges of high treason in 1681 and honored by a medal struck to commemorate the event. *MacFlecknoe* (1685) lampoons minor poet Thomas Shadwell outrageously in a mock-heroic poem. After becoming a Roman Catholic, Dryden wrote *The Hind and the Panther* to reconcile Anglican and Catholic political interests while defending Catholic doctrine.

Occasional poetry: Named Poet Laureate in 1668, Dryden had long written poems to commemorate great occasions. Three examples are *Heroic Stanzas* (1659), on the death of Cromwell; *Annus Mirabilis* (1667), celebrating the English naval victory over the Dutch and the fortitude of Londoners in sustaining the Great Fire; and *On the Death of Mr. Henry Purcell* (1686), memorializing England's greatest composer.

The great odes: These include *Song for St. Cecilia's Day* (1687), which has an unusually rich-toned majesty, and *Alexander's Feast* (1697), which was given a famous musical setting by Handel.

Key 43   The satire of Swift

OVERVIEW *Jonathan Swift (1667–1745), a controver-sial clergyman, is the foremost prose satirist of English lit-erature.*

Attitude: A man of social charm and a friend of Addison, Pope, John Gay, and many other writers, Swift also had a darker side that led some scholars to think (wrongly) that his great satires were the prod-ucts of a diseased mind. He was, however, a misanthrope; in a letter to Pope he wrote that though he loved individuals, he hated mankind in general.

Early prose works: During the years 1696–98 Swift wrote two impor-tant satires.

- *A Tale of a Tub* (1696) burlesques church history and dogma in a narrative about three brothers: Peter (standing for Roman Catho-lics), Martin (Lutherans or Anglicans), and Jack (extreme Protes-tants). They each inherit coats, with the injunction that they are not to be altered in any way. They gradually disobey, finding fanciful excuses for adding shoulder-knots or gold lace, according to the current fashion (just as orthodox churchmen find ways to modify their doctrines).

- *The Battle of the Books* (1697) is a prose mock-epic that satirizes conflict between advocates of modern and of ancient literature. It opens with a dispute arising between a spider and a bee entangled in the spider's web. Aesop sums up the dispute: the spider is like the moderns who spin their scholastic lore out of their own entrails; the bee is like the ancients, who go to nature for their honey.

Journal to Stella (1710–13): A volume of intimate letters to Esther Johnson and her duenna, it gives vivid pictures of daily life in London and gossip about political intrigues. He is at his playful best writing, sometimes in baby language, to a woman whom he met as a child, educated, grew to love, and may have secretly married.

Gulliver's Travels (1726): Swift's most universal satire, and still popu-lar today, it adopts the ancient device of an imaginary voyage, with Gulliver travelling to four "remote nations of the world," enabling Swift to approach the foibles to mankind from a fresh viewpoint.

- In Part I Gulliver visits Lilliput, where the natives are only six inches tall. Their foolish pretensions caricature the disputes of contemporary England.

- Part II reverses the situation—Brobdingnag has natives sixty feet tall—but again the pretensions and preoccupations of England and humanity in general are ridiculed.
- In Part III Gulliver visits Laputa, a land where scholars and scientists are involved in esoteric and unimportant projects.
- In Part IV, which is the most widely applicable satire, he visits the kingdom of the Houyhnhnms, intelligent horses who are beset by dirty, ignorant, and perverse human-like creatures called Yahoos.

Features of Swift's satires:
- Universal, attacking all things human.
- Elemental, gigantic power.
- Bitter, almost insane scorn.
- Clean-cut, precise style.
- Coarse humor, tinged with irony.

Later occasional pieces: The best-known is *Modest Proposal for Preventing the Children of Poor People from Being a Burden to Their Parents or Country* (1729). In this savage satire (in which he hoped to dramatize the misery of the Irish poor), he advocates selling Irish babies for food for the wealthy classes. The four-volume *Miscellanies* (1727–32), assembled by Pope from writings by the Scriblerus Club, is dominated by short essays by Swift.

Last works: Some of his most famous tracts and characteristic poems were written during his last years, in Ireland: *The Grand Question Debated* (1729); *Verses on the Death of Dr. Swift* (1731), in which he reviews his life and work with humor; and the ironical *Directions to Servants* (1731, published posthumously).

Key 44 The essays of Addison and Steele

OVERVIEW *For the first time, prose began to excel poetry in quantity and quality in the early part of the 18th century.*

Periodicals: Londoners gathered in the popular coffee-houses to read the news sheets and the literary periodicals. The best were *The Tatler* (1709) and *The Spectator* (1711), written primarily by **Joseph Addison** (1672–1719) and **Richard Steele** (1672–1729), two powerful influences on the English prose style.

Addison: His literary fame comes almost entirely from his periodical essays on literature and the foibles of society.
- **Literary criticism**: His most original contributions were eleven *Spectator* papers on the "Pleasures of the Imagination," stating that imaginative feelings are stimulated by "what is great, uncommon, or beautiful." He also wrote papers on Milton, intelligently analyzing and praising that author.
- **Social criticism**: The announced purpose of the *Spectator* was to "enliven morality with wit, and to temper wit with morality." Materialism and superficiality were satirized in vivid pictures of city life, e.g. Sir Roger's visit to Westminster Abbey, and country life, e.g. Sir Roger at the assizes.
- **Sir Roger de Coverley Papers**: Like a novel, with each essay on Sir Roger a separate chapter, these papers could have been a serial story with the addition of more plot structure.

Steele: Though he seems to have had more originality, conceiving the idea of the *Tatler* and *Spectator* (and even the character Sir Roger), he lacked Addison's shrewd wit and literary craftsmanship. Though Steele lacks the elegance and correctness of Addison, he writes warmer, more emotional prose. John Gay liked his essays under the pen name "Bickerstaff," saying they set "men of letters upon a new way of thinking."
- His sentimental dramas were described by Fielding's fictional Parson Adams as "almost solemn enough for a sermon."
- His essays include an attack on Restoration drama, several praising family life, and one expressing approval of the "sober and polite Mirth" of the Roman playwright Terence.

Key 45   Defoe and the birth of the novel

OVERVIEW   *Though there had been lengthy prose fiction—often disguised as allegory—in the Renaissance, it was not until the 18th century that the **novel** emerged as a form with tight structure and an interplay between individuals and their relationships to society.*

Daniel Defoe (1659–1731): He wrote what is often called the first English novel, ***Robinson Crusoe***. Defoe's method was somewhat journalistic; his narratives are always fictional autobiographies pretending to be true. He did not fully understand the complex possibilities of structure in the novel, but he created a variety of superbly detailed episodes.

- ***Robinson Crusoe*** (1719) is a fictional grafting on the adventures of the shipwrecked Alexander Selkirk, whose return to London caused a journalistic furor. Four editions were published in four months.
- ***The Fortunes and Misfortunes of Moll Flanders*** (1722), describing Moll's amours when young and thievery when middle-aged, is more like a modern novel because a nucleus of a social group is reunited in the end. Most 18th century novels follow one character through a series of adventures in the **picaresque** manner.
- ***A Journal of the Plague Year*** (1722) turns history into fiction as Defoe creates an imaginary narrator-observer who records in his diary the terrible year in which 70,000 Londoners died of the bubonic plague.

Defoe's versatility: No English writer has been more prolific and wide-ranging than Defoe. He produced some 560 books, pamphlets, and journals, many anonymously and pseudonymously.

Minor novelists: A popular genre in fiction was the "scandal chronicles," gossip stories about the upper classes, with names concealed transparently under pseudonyms. **Mrs. Mary Delariviere Manley** (1663–1724), an early leader in the genre, wrote *Secret Memoirs and Manners of Several Persons of Quality* (1709–10), a bold satire. **Mrs. Eliza Haywood** (c.1693–1756) wrote *Memoirs of Utopia* (2 vols., 1725) in the same vein.

Key 46   Richardson: New direction for the novel

OVERVIEW   *In the final analysis, Defoe's novels lacked plot. The first novel to be guided throughout by a single motif—love—was* Pamela, *written by a London printer, Samuel Richardson (1689–1761).*

Epistolary novel: Richardson wrote all his works in the epistolary form (i.e., made up of letters). He liked the immediacy of the form and called it "writing to the moment."

Pamela (1740): Its origin was unusual. Richardson had been asked to write a volume of letters as models of correspondence and behavior. To add interest, he wrote them as letters from a servant-girl to her parents, containing long transcripts of conversations. Pamela is sexually harassed by her master, but she resists and finally succeeds in marrying him. The letters are more like detailed journals than models of correspondence. The novel had a great popularity on the Continent and was soon adapted for the stage in France.

Clarissa (8 vols., 1747–48): Richardson's second novel, it followed the great popularity of *Pamela*. Also told in letters, the story is somewhat more complex, with a love triangle involving Clarissa and two suitors. Clarissa Harlowe is a member of an acquisitive, ambitious, "narrow-souled" middle class family, which decides that Lovelace is not good enough and that she should marry the wealthy Solmes.

Sir Charles Grandison (1753–54): The hero (Richardson's portrayal of the "good man") must decide which of two young ladies would make the appropriate wife. It satirizes the upper and middle classes, of which Richardson had little first-hand knowledge.

Richardson's moral tone: Being of the middle class, Richardson understood well their two principal preoccupations: deportment and conscience. His novels were to be instructive of the art of living in several contexts: Pamela is a model servant, Clarissa exemplifies the higher class, and Sir Charles illustrates the adaptation of aristocratic manners to middle-class instincts.

Key 47 The novels of Fielding and Smollett

OVERVIEW *Richardson's moral pretensions led **Henry Fielding** (1707–1754) to become a novelist. Perceiving Pamela as overly sentimental and ethically shallow, he began to write a burlesque of it in the form of a picaresque novel. **Tobias Smollett** (1721–1771) also wrote picaresque novels which featured a roguish hero on the road to a succession of escapades, but both authors advanced the novel to a higher plane.*

Fielding's novels: Though of a higher class than Richardson, Fielding's books show a dislike of high society; he wrote in ***Tom Jones*** that "the highest life is much the dullest, and affords little humor or entertainment." He cared little for the rewards of virtue, believing poverty and contempt as likely to be virtue's rewards as happiness. These attitudes and his use of the patterns of the prose epic are his chief contributions to the novel form.

- ***Joseph Andrews*** (1742), in its original form, was a burlesque of Richarson's *Pamela,* entitled *Shamela,* in which Pamela's brother Joseph is sexually harassed by his mistress. Highly indecent for that era, Fielding refined it into the more truly comic *Joseph Andrews*. Parson Adams, the first of Fielding's portraits of the "good man," has long been a favorite.

- ***The Life and Death of Jonathan Wild the Great*** (1743) is a shorter, looser narrative, more typically picaresque. The subject is a notorious rogue, allowing Fielding to satirize the exaggeration practiced by most biographers as he holds Wild up for admiration for his clever practice of cruelty, corruption, and greed.

KEY QUOTATION

He in a few minutes ravished this fair creature, or at least would have ravished her, if she had not, by a timely compliance, prevented him.

Jonathan Wild

- ***The History of Tom Jones, a Foundling*** (1749) is Fielding's acknowledged masterpiece, a "comic epic poem in prose," and one of the best-plotted English novels. Each episode contributes to the general—and intricate—narrative pattern. Philosophically, Fielding still believes that virtue is easily deceived, and Tom's adventures allow Fielding to express a jaundiced view of all levels of English society.

- *Amelia* (1751), a novel of London life, is grim in tone, lacking the high spirits and nimble wit of the others. There is no catharsis for the scenes of extreme poverty and the general hardness of life.

Assessment of Fielding's fiction: Modern critics declare him to be an innovative writer of the highest originality. He thought of himself, rightly, as "the founder of a new province of writing." Sir Walter Scott praised him for his "high notions of the dignity of an art which he may be considered as having founded."

Smollett's novels: A Scotsman who failed at the profession of surgery because of his irascible temper, Smollett wrote narratives that, perhaps predictably, lack human sympathy. His novels excel in striking human detail rather than in plot structure. Like Fielding, he was a critic of aristocratic manners, but he knew little of the upper classes firsthand.

- *Roderick Random* (1748) is a true picaresque novel, a succession of adventures narrated by the hero. Its greatest virtue is graphic detail, especially in describing Roderick's life as a surgeon's mate aboard a naval ship. In his preface, Smollett declared his purpose to be to arouse "generous indignation... against the vicious disposition of the world."

KEY QUOTATION

I was often inhumanly scourged for crimes I did not commit; because, having the character of a vagabond in the village, every piece of mischief, whose author lay unknown, was charged upon me. I have been found guilty of robbing orchards I never entered, of killing cats I never hurted, or stealing gingerbread I never touched, and of abusing old women I never saw.

—Roderick Random

- *Peregrine Pickle* (1751) is precisely the same sort of picaresque novel except that the hero is English, not Scottish, and the tale is told by the author as narrator, not in the first person. The principal target of the satire seems to be Pride, in all its many forms.
- *The Expedition of Humphrey Clinker* (1771) is Smollett's last novel and his masterpiece. He hated the mannered activities at Bath and other watering holes and is ingenious in devising ways to satirize them. He discards his previous narrative method and uses the epistolary form masterfully.

Key 48   Sterne's controversial novels

OVERVIEW   *The orderly, suspenseful structure of novels by Fielding led the virtuoso author* Lawrence Sterne *(1713– 1768) to experiment with form, setting, and new types of comic subject matter.*

Tone: Although Sterne was a clergyman, he had a penchant for gross and indecent humor; his friends tried to help him curb his salacious bent.

Sterne's works: His career was short, and his work, though significant in literary history, is limited to seven small volumes of *Sermons* (1760–69); his correspondence, including *Letters from Yorick to Eliza* (1773); and two works of fiction:
- *The Life and Times of Tristram Shandy* (1759–67) is a chaotic novel, with digressions stemming from digressions. It is obsessed with minute detail that seems to have little continuity. Unbearable, were Sterne not a genius who made comedy from the association of ideas and the idiosyncracies of character. He uses outrageous tricks: blank pages, black pages, and the placing of the Preface in the middle of the book. There are recurrent indecent associations and innuendos.
- *A Sentimental Journey Through France and Italy* (1768) answers the adverse criticism of *Tristram Shandy* with a more elegant, less grotesque book. The comedy is tenderer and the overall design is to "teach us to love the world and our fellow creatures better than we do." Though Sterne makes little use of the ordinary material of novelists—desires, passions, political or religious beliefs, success and failure—he has the power of imparting humanity to his eccentric characters.
- **Sterne's legacy**: This innovator is now assumed to be the founding father of a long line of writers interested in the "stream of consciousness." The idea came from philosophy; in *Tristram Shandy* Sterne acknowledges a debt to John Locke's *Essay Concerning Human Understanding,* which seemed to Sterne a "history-book . . . of what passes in man's own mind." One of the most delightful aspects of his fiction are the ingenious parodies of the developing cliches in the still-new novel form.

Key 49 Pope and Neoclassicism

OVERVIEW *Alexander Pope (1688–1744) was the most brilliant man of letters in the early 18th century, but his art and genius were limited by the Neoclassical emphasis on being correct in following the rules of art, on expressing universal truths rather than personal emotion, and in using exclusively the heroic couplet rather than the more liberating poetic forms.*

Literary criticism: *An Essay on Criticism* (1711), written when Pope was quite young, is full of polished epigrams—in heroic couplets—about writing in the Neoclassical style. He defines **"true wit"** in the poem as "What oft was thought, but ne'er so well expressed." In three parts, the poem explores the relationship of "wit" and art in writing poetry, discusses the nature of false "wit," and defines the attributes of the good literary critic, who should read each work in the spirit in which the author intended it. Remarkably, he wrote the poem at age 21.

Satire: Some of Pope's best—and best known—poetry is in his satires.
- *The Rape of the Lock* (1712–14) is a "mock epic," a comic poem with an exaggerated epic form, but trivial subject. It is based on an actual quarrel between two families, resulting from Lord Petre's clipping a lock of Miss Arabella's hair. Dr. Samuel Johnson called it "the most attractive of all ludicrous compositions."
- *The Dunciad* (1728) is modeled after Dryden's *Macflecknoe* (Key 42), but it is even more elaborate in its mock-epic framework and witty allusions to "dunces" (his literary rivals). Not only does Pope satirize all authors who have earned his condemnation, he exposes all literary and stylistic abuses and holds them up to ridicule.
- *Epistle to Dr. Arbuthnot* (1734-35), Pope's most polished work, defends the art of satire and attacks such authors as Joseph Addison and Lady Mary Wortley Montagu.

Philosophical poetry: *Essay on Man* (1733) deals with the existence of evil in a world created by a benevolent God, finally asserting that evil is a necessity and that "whatever is, is right."

Key 50   Boswell and the early biographers

OVERVIEW   *James Boswell (1740–1795), called the "Shakespeare of biographers" by Macaulay, had a great biographical subject: Dr. Samuel Johnson (Key 51).*

Works: Innovatively, Boswell attempted a complete portrayal of Johnson: his foibles, his virtues, his genius, and his marvelously quotable comments. The discovery in the 20th century of his journals gave Boswell an enhanced reputation as one of the world's great diarists.

The Life of Samuel Johnson, LL.D. (1791): Boswell made important decisions as he began writing this new kind of biography. He decided:

- that the "extraordinary vigor and vivacity of Johnson's mind" was his most significant characteristic.
- that he would tell the truth, presenting his subject as he was.
- to step back as much as possible and let the drama itself come forward.
- not to exclude details, but present them minutely.

Boswell's special talents: He has a prodigious memory, rarely making notes of conversations, but recording them later in accurate remembrance. Though not a trained scholar, he was remarkably thorough and was ingenious in structuring the biography. Such scenes as Boswell's first meeting with Johnson or the famous dinner with Wilkes are masterpieces of theatrical manipulation.

Boswell's other works: Those published during his lifetime included *An Account of Corsica* (1768) and *Journal of a Tour of the Hebrides* (1785). From 1777 to 1783 he contributed a series of essays as "The Hypochondriack" to *The London Magazine* on the subjects of drinking, diaries, memory, and hypochondria.

Other early biographers: Before Boswell; biographies were thin, dry, and factual—*Life of Francis Bacon* (1740) by David Mallet, *Sir Thomas More* (1758) by Ferdinando Warner, and *Erasmus* (1758–60) by John Jortin—or anecdotal sketches like John Aubrey's *Brief Lives* (1690).

Key 51 Samuel Johnson, man of letters

OVERVIEW *Samuel Johnson (1709–84) is revealed in Boswell's biography (Key 50) as a wise and witty conversationalist with many eccentricities. He is seen also as a great man of letters: a poet, an accomplished scholar, the greatest literary critic of the 18th century, and a prose stylist of extraordinary directness and balance.*

Dictionary: The publication of Johnson's *Dictionary of the English Language* (1755) was the most important linguistic event of the 18th century; it "fixed" English spelling and established a standard for definition. With the help of six assistants, the volume was completed in slightly over eight years. It includes such famous definitions as the one for *network:* "anything reticulated or decussated, at equal distances, with interstices between the intersections."

Shakespeare: Johnson's long-awaited edition of Shakespeare's plays appeared in 1765. The work, which interpreted the plays and suggested sources of the plots, greatly stimulated Shakespearean scholarship.

Literary criticism: His last and best work was *Lives of the English Poets* (1779–81), which gives biographical sketches, critical judgments, and criticism of the individual works of 52 poets. There are brilliant insights and some faulty judgments based on personal bias; for example, he disliked Milton for his religious and political beliefs. He believes that the main aim of poetry is "to instruct by pleasing."

Moralistic prose:
- *The Vision of Theodore, the Hermit of Teneriffe* (1748) was considered by Johnson to be the best thing he ever wrote. This moral allegory questions whether habitual worship deadens religious sincerity.
- *History of Rasselas, Prince of Abyssinia* (1779), a philosophical romance, is his most appealing statement of his ideas on the vanity of human wishes, on the impossibility of complete happiness in the imperfect world of humankind.

Key 52   Three 18th Century comic dramatists

OVERVIEW   *Drama in the early 18th century was primarily **sentimental comedy**, called "weeping comedy," but the popularity of a satiric ballad opera by Gay and the subsequent anti-sentimental plays of Goldsmith and Sheridan revived a satirical comedy of manners.*

John Gay (1685–1732): He wrote the first ballad opera—a precursor of modern muscial comedy—***The Beggar's Opera*** (1728), the most popular theatrical work of the 18th century. In it, thieves and strumpets mimic and burlesque the manners of fine lords and ladies, allowing Gay to satirize the inequalities of social classes.

Oliver Goldsmith (1728–1774): He was the author of three very popular 18th century works: the poem **"The Deserted Village"** (1770), the novel ***The Vicar of Wakefield*** (1776), and the comic drama ***She Stoops to Conquer*** (1771). His poem bemoans the loss of wholesome village life due to Enclosure Laws and the Industrial Revolution. The novel describes the vicar, Dr. Primrose, as combining the "three greatest characters upon earth; he is a priest, a husbandman, and the father of a family." In the play, he avoids sentimentality in a witty comedy about a bashful suitor who overcomes shyness when he mistakes a lady of fashion for a barmaid.

Richard Brinsley Sheridan (1751–1816): Less idealistic in his outlook than Goldsmith, his plays reflect the satiric observation of life found in 18th century novels. They are witty, elegant comedies, purged of Restoration indecencies.
- ***The Rivals*** (1775), written when Sheridan was 20, is known for its famous character Mrs. Malaprop, whose fractured phrases have since been known as "malapropisms." She advocates, for example, that a young lady be "instructed in geometry, that she might know something of the contagious countries."
- ***The School for Scandal*** (1777) is a brilliantly written play, abounding in elegantly stated wit, with a well-manipulated intrigue that leads to a famous scene involving a screen. Sheridan is particularly cutting to the sentimentalists in this play as he gives his audience the sleazy quintessence of a scandal-loving society.

Key 53   The Pre-Romantic poets

OVERVIEW   *In the latter half of the 18th century poets began turning away from the rationalistic Neoclassical norms and the limiting couplet verse form. They turned to the picturesque aspects of nature, melancholy emotions, medieval literature and architecture, and the virtues of rural life.*

James Thomson (1700–48): *The Seasons* (1730) is a blank verse poem about the changing tapestry of nature throughout the year. *The Castle of Indolence* (1748) gently mocks the poet's love of idleness and contains a portrait of himself: ''A bard here dwelt, more fat than bard beseems.''

Thomas Gray (1716–71): Among his few poems is **''The Elegy Written in a Country Churchyard''** (1751), one of the best-known English poems. Though marred by Neoclassical personifications and cliches, it glorifies simple rural folk as does Wordsworth (Key 56) later in the Romantic Period. His first ode, ''Ode on a Distant Prospect of Eton College'' (1747), observes schoolboys at a distance, happily playing, unmindful of future sadness, and he warns, ''If ignorance is bliss, 'tis folly to be wise.''

William Collins (1721–59): ''A precursor of Keats (Key 60), Collins was one of the most original poets of his day, using elegant, precise imagery in his imaginative depiction of the more somber aspects of nature in his best-known poem ''Ode to Evening.''

William Cowper (1731–1800): He was influential in turning public taste toward the Romanticism of the 19th century writers. Cowper's best-known work is *The Task* (1785), a volume of poems with the express purpose of proving the superiority of ''rural ease and leisure'' over London life for living a life of virtue. He had a keen eye and whimsical humor; he was self-revealing with an intimacy that was foreign to Neoclassical writers. He wrote **''The Castaway''** shortly before his death. The poignant lyric deals with man's isolation and helplessness. He was a champion of the oppressed, and he wrote complimentary verses on William Wilberforce and his opposition to the slave trade.

Theme 7 THE ROMANTIC
PERIOD

*M*ost historians of English literature mark the beginning of the Romantic Period as 1798, when Wordsworth and Coleridge changed the course of English poetry by publishing *Lyrical Ballads*. The ending is usually 1832, the year Sir Walter Scott died. The year 1832 also brought the first Reform Bill, signifying the Victorian readjustment of political power in recognition of the rising middle class. In that short time England changed from a predominantly rural, agricultural society to an urban industrial one. It was a time of liberal thought; most of the Romantic writers had come of age in the aftermath of the revolutions in America and France, and they held human rights dear. The rise of Napolean, his growing empire, and his defeat at Waterloo are among the historical events that most strongly affected the literature of the period.

Key 54   Characteristics of the Romantic period

OVERVIEW   *Romanticism was born in a turbulent age that saw three revolutions—the American (1776), the French (1798), and the Industrial (1770s to the present). Revolutionary tendencies also affected poetry as Wordsworth, Coleridge, Blake, Shelley, Keats, and Byron abandoned strict Neoclassical formalism and profoundly changed the nature of English literature.*

Revolutionary age: Wordsworth was 19 when the French Revolution erupted, and for him it was "bliss" to be alive at a time when "liberty, equality, and fraternity" came to the forefront. All the other major Romantic poets except Keats were avidly political, championing human rights in their poetry. Lord Byron's first speech in the House of Lords defended some poor weavers, casualties in the Industrial Revolution.

Reinterpreting the past: To the 18th century authors, medievalism had suggested barbarism, superstition, and ignorance. The Romantics looked back at the Middle Ages and saw an age of faith, idealism, and adventure. For example, the basic medieval element, the quest romance, was used to show an internal quest for self-knowledge in Wordsworth's *Prelude* (Key 56), Coleridge's *Rime of the Ancient Mariner* (Key 57), and Shelley's *Prometheus Unbound* (Key 59).

New literary theory: Wordsworth advocated poetry written in the language really used by simple rural folk, and he dared to use subject matter that was "common" and considered "unpoetical." Although the poet had a heightened sensitivity, he did not elevate himself above his reader, but spoke as a "man speaking to men."

General features of romantic poetry: Usually found are references to nature and natural objects, intimate self-revelation of the poet, and direct expression of emotions. The imagery reflects a careful attention to concrete particulars.

Key 55   Blake and Burns

OVERVIEW   *Two dissimilar poets were powerful influences early in the Romantic Period: **William Blake**, a mystic, other-worldly poet and painter, and **Robert Burns**, a
Scottish peasant-poet who achieved greater fame than Blake
in his lifetime.*

William Blake (1757–1827): He broke with Neoclassicism as early as
1789 with his simple—but psychological—lyrics of innocence and
experience, and he continued in the Romantic vein with his complex
long poems, "prophetic works" that were made difficult by Blake's
private mythology.
- *Songs of Innocence* (1789–90) and *Songs of Experience* (1794):
  To publish these short poems, Blake engraved the text and accom-
  panying drawings on copper plates. These simple, imaginative
  lyrics show Blake's compassion for the poor and his hatred of
  repression.
- *The Marriage of Heaven and Hell* (1790–93) attacks sexual and
  social morality as interpreted by organized religion because it
  restrains creative energy and genius. The section "Proverbs of
  Hell" is especially striking.
- *The Book of Urizen* (1794), a complex poem about the fall of
  man, uses Blake's Mythology: Urizen is reason, Los is imagination, and Orc is libido.
- *The Four Zoas* (c. 1797–1804), an epic of 3,600 lines, narrates
  the fall and restoration of "eternal man."

Robert Burns (1759–96): Beginning as a folk-rhymer in Scottish dia-
lect, Burns became increasingly sophisticated, producing biting sat-
ires and songs of love, nature, and rural life.
- **Satires**: "Holy Willie's Prayer," "Address to the Unco Guid,"
  and "The Holy Fair" are directed at religious hypocrites and strict
  Calvinists.
- **Songs**: Much admired are the light-hearted love songs ("Highland
  Mary" and "A Red, Red Rose"), drinking songs ("Willie
  Brewed a Peck o' Maut"), and stirring democratic lyrics ("A
  Man's a Man for A' That").
- **Longer Poems**: "Tam O'Shanter," a rollicking narrative of a
  drunken adventure, and "The Cotter's Saturday Night," an affec-
  tionate picture of rural life, are typical.

Key 56 Wordsworth and his revolutionary theory of poetry

OVERVIEW *William Wordsworth (1770–1850) found the poetry of the Neoclassical period too artificial, too rhetorical in language, too restrained in its expression of emotion, and too repressive of the imagination. His theories changed the face of poetry.*

Lyrical Ballads (1798): Wordsworth and his friend **Samuel Taylor Coleridge** (Key 57) conceived this volume as an experiment in poetry to determine ''how far the language of conversation in the middle and lower classes of society is adapted to the purposes of poetic pleasure.''

Theory: In a later preface to that volume, Wordsworth wrote that the ''passions'' exist in their purest form in simple rural life, and thus in his new kind of poetry the humble activities of ordinary people can serve as poetic themes. His lyrical ballads contain sincere and deeply felt responses to the beauties of nature, following his belief that poetry is ''the spontaneous overflow of powerful feelings'' that are ''recollected in tranquility.''

Poet of nature and the people: This genius of simple tastes loved his native Lake District in northwest England and the yeoman farmers and shepherds there. He combined the new revolutionary attitudes about freedom and social classes with his new approach to literature.

His greatest poem: Wordsworth's masterwork, **The Prelude**, a massive blank-verse autobiography of his poetic mind, was revised over a period of fifty years and published a few months before his death in 1850. Many critics consider it the century's greatest poem.

Nature poems: Even more readers are moved by his simple lyrics of nature, describing such delights as a field of daffodils, an unexpected rainbow, fields on a sunny morning following a stormy night. He contrasts the harmony and peace of nature with the cruelty human beings inflict upon each other.

Key 57 Coleridge: Poet, critic, and visionary

OVERVIEW *Samuel Taylor Coleridge (1772–1834) was a collaborator with Wordsworth on the* Lyrical Ballads *(Key 56), but more importantly he defended this new approach to poetry in the significant critical work* Biographia Literaria. *Coleridge was an innovative poet, writing strange poems of the supernatural as well as personal meditations called "conversation poems."*

Supernatural poems: Among his crowning achievements are **"Kubla Khan,"** a fragment of fantastic imagery based on an opium-induced dream, and two powerful narratives of romantic witchery:

- **"The Rime of the Ancient Mariner"** is a parable of a seaman's crime against nature (pointlessly killing an albatross) and his repentance by blessing the lowly water-snakes. Setting the poem in the Middle Ages in the then-unknown seas near Antarctica, the poet is able to make his narrative credible and give the reader what he called "the willing suspension of disbelief."
- **"Christabel"** is an unfinished tale of a witch, Geraldine, entering the life of the beautiful maiden Christabel, even to the point of inhabiting her lover's body.

Conversation poems: These were quiet, descriptive, highly personal poems in a form originated and perfected by Coleridge. Realistic imagery of rural life is found in **"Frost at Midnight"** and **"This Lime Tree Bower My Prison."**

Literary Criticism: Coleridge's *Biographia Literaria* (1817), his most important work in prose, contains autobiography, literary criticism, and philosophy. His sections on the superiority of imagination over mere logic are classics, as are the analyses of literary works by Wordsworth and Shakespeare.

Influence: Perhaps even more important than his writings was his influence on a new generation of writers who listened intently to one who had mastered nearly every important work of literature. He also gave many important public lectures, particularly on the plays of Shakespeare.

Key 58   Byron: Neoclassical and Romantic poet

OVERVIEW   *Although* **George Gordon, Lord Byron** *(1788–1824) was more Neoclassical than romantic in his earliest poems, he was to become—primarily because of his image as a proud, mysterious young aristocrat—the personification of romanticism. He wrote a large and remarkably varied body of poetry; some works have taken surprising upturns in evaluation, while others have been devalued.*

Satires: The Neoclassical satire *English Bards and Scotch Reviewers* (1808) attacks the poetry of Wordsworth, Coleridge, and Southey in Popean heroic couplets. One of his last poems, *The Vision of Judgment* (1822), blasts these same poets.

Poetic travelogue: *Childe Harold's Pilgrimage* (1809–17) establishes the Byronic hero, a moody, cynical commentator who is traveling through Europe. After a public scandal involving Byron's half-sister, the third and fourth cantos have "self-exiled Harold" mouthing the poet's bitter invective against English society.

Manfred, A Dramatic Poem (1816–17): This **closet drama** has a young Byronic hero with a dark secret of forbidden love. It has been compared with Marlowe's *Dr. Faustus* (Key 37).

Don Juan: This unfinished masterpiece has sixteen completed cantos of a comic epic that is unsurpassed in English literature for its glorious mixture of realism integrated with romance and sentiment enlivened by buffoonery. There are two main characters: the legendary lover Don Juan and the gossipy, worldly-wise narrator, who uses puns, outrageous rhymes, and a wry view of human society to make every ottava rima stanza verbally interesting. The "anti-Romantic" Dedication attacks Wordsworth, Coleridge, and Southey for dullness and ambiguity.

Byron's impact on Europe: He supported the Greeks in their war for independence from the Turks. He sailed to Greece with money and medical supplies in 1823, and he died there shortly afterwards from a fever. Such activities made him a hero in Europe, where his poetry is perhaps overly praised.

Key 59   Shelley: Poet and political
rebel

OVERVIEW   *The life and poetry of the aristocratic **Percy
Bysshe Shelley** (1792–1822) was marked by revolutionary
fervor and radical idealism joined with great literary talents.*

Shelley: No other English poet can match him for pure lyric genius.
Though only 29 when he drowned, Shelley accomplished much, progressing from pamphlets on the cause of Irish freedom to the magnificent verse drama ***Prometheus Unbound***, the supreme expression
in literature of the perfectibility of the human race. Platonic idealism
provides the intellectual background for many of his poems.

- ***Queen Mab*** (1813) is a visionary poem that presents some of
  Shelley's most revolutionary ideas: his dislike for tyranny and
  orthodox Christianity, as well as his belief that mankind is moving
  steadily toward perfection.
- ***Alastor*** (1815) is a blank verse allegory of the poet's quest for the
  ideal woman, Shelley's first major poem.
- "**Mont Blanc**" and "**Hymn to Intellectual Beauty**" (both 1816)
  are idealistic companion poems; in them Shelley attempts to convey an idea of the ultimate Being or Power of the universe.
- "**Ode to the West Wind**" (1819) depicts the dual nature of the
  West Wind, as both destroyer and preserver, blowing away the
  leaves, but scattering the seeds for a rebirth.
- "**To a Skylark**" (1820), Shelley's most popular lyric, uses ingenious imagery to convey the "spirit" of this songbird and compare
  its role to that of the poet.
- ***Adonais*** (1821), a pastoral elegy on the death of Keats, adapts the
  myth of Adonis's death in celebrating Keats's rebirth into an ideal
  Platonic world.
- ***Prometheus Unbound*** (1818) is Shelley's masterpiece, a lyric
  drama in four acts that uses the myth of the chained titan to portray
  the ultimate resistance to tyranny, leading to a perfected world.

Shelley's reputation today: The ethereal qualities of Shelley's poetry,
his breadth of intellect, his musical lyricism, and his unique feeling
for the most impalpable aspects of nature place him in the front rank
of English poets.

Key 60   Keats: A Romantic symbol

OVERVIEW   *Dying at 25 after a brief poetic career, John Keats (1795–1821) was richly endowed with the talents that produce major poetry: effortless magic of phrase, agile use of poetic styles, and a wide range of sympathetic understanding.*

"Year of Miracles": In 1819, despite serious illness and an unresolved love affair, Keats wrote his six great odes, *The Eve of St. Agnes,* and a group of excellent sonnets in nine marvelous months.

The sonnets: Keats wrote highly personal sonnets that include "On Seeing the Elgin Marbles" and "On First Looking Into Chapman's Homer," conveying his joy at experiencing art.

Long Poems: *Endymion* (1817) is remembered for the line "A thing of beauty is a joy forever" and for the belief that critical attacks on the poem led to Keats's early death. *The Eve of St. Agnes* (1819) is a narrative in Spenserian stanzas with unusually delicate and sensuous imagery.

The great odes: These six poems, written in 1819, show Keats's remarkable maturity as a poet, his use of all his senses in his concrete imagery, and his ability to lose his own identity in contemplating the external world (an ability he called *Negative Capability*).

- *Ode to Psyche:* Psyche, a mortal who wins a place on Mount Olympus, has no temple; Keats will be her priest and build her temple "in some untrodden region" of his mind.
- *Ode to a Nightingale:* Listening in darkness to the notes of a nightingale, Keats wishes to blend with the bird, to leave this sad and forever-changing earth.
- *Ode on a Grecian Urn:* Keats is comforted by the realization that ideal art is truth and that art is permanent.
- *Ode on Melancholy:* Do not seek to escape melancholy by poison; indulge in melancholy, "glut" yourself in it, and it will be as transitory as beauty.
- *Ode on Indolence:* This fanciful poem depicts three allegorical figures circling before the poet, temporarily indolent, blocked from poetic expression.
- *To Autumn:* This ode gloriously evokes the fall season, with some of Keats's finest nature imagery.

Key 61   Prose essayists of the Romantic period

OVERVIEW   *Although poetry was the most important literary medium of the Romantic Period, an innovation in prose—the **personal essay**—was also significant.*

The personal essay: The essayists DeQuincey, Hazlitt, and Lamb abandoned the traditions of the formal essay for this more impressionistic, less structured essay that disclosed more of the personality of the writer.

Thomas DeQuincey (1785–1859): His *Confessions of An English Opium Eater* (1821) is written in a sensuous, imaginative style, revealing his addiction in intimate detail.

Literary criticism: In "The poetry of Pope" DeQuincey distinguished between the "literature of knowledge," which teaches, and the "literature of power," which moves the emotions. His essay "On the Knocking at the Gate in *Macbeth*" explains one of Shakespeare's great subtleties of staging as the audience is skillfully returned to the real world after the horrendous murder scene.

William Hazlitt (1778–1830): Along with Coleridge he was considered one of the most important literary critics of the day. Hazlitt's *The Characters of Shakespeare's Plays* was significant, as were his numerous essays on Elizabethan playwrights.

Popular essays: Hazlitt's "My First Acquaintance with Poets" (about meeting Wordsworth and Coleridge), "On Going on a Journey," and "The Fight" (about a brutal bare-knuckle bout) appeared first in collections entitled *Table Talk* and were popular for their interesting details set in narrative frameworks.

Charles Lamb (1775–1834): Greatest of the personal essayists, he was praised for his lucid style, emotional warmth, and wry sense of humor.

Essays of Elia (1823–33): This two-volume collection of Lamb's work includes "The Two Races of Men" (borrowers and lenders), "Poor Relations" (a keen insight into family relationship), and "Old China" (a nostalgic look at younger, poorer days, when he could afford only the second-balcony seats at the theater).

Key 62   Major novelists: Jane Austen and Sir Walter Scott

OVERVIEW   *The novels of the Romantic period fall into four general categories: the Gothic Romance (**Mrs. Anne Radcliffe's** The Mysteries of Udolpho, 1794), the novel of purpose (**William Godwin's** Caleb Williams, 1794), the novel of manners (**Jane Austen**), and historical novels (popularized by **Sir Walter Scott**).*

Jane Austen (1775–1817): The greatest novelist of the period, she transcends the genre *novel of manners* (concerned with the manners and customs of a specific social class) with her gentle but satirical wit, the clarity of her insights into human nature, and her lucid, delicately balanced style.
- *Sense and Sensibility* (pub. 1811) satirizes the sentimental traditions of love (as displayed by the emotional heroine, Marianne).
- *Pride and Prejudice* (pub. 1813) features her best-loved character, Elizabeth Bennet, whom Austen called "as delightful a creature as ever appeared in print." The efforts of the dotty Mrs. Bennet to see her daughters well married conveys much of the satire.
- *Emma* (pub. 1815) has two great comic creations, Mr. Woodhouse and Miss Bates. Emma is said to be the most profound of Jane Austen's characterizations, although the author described her as "a heroine whom no one but myself will like very much."

Sir Walter Scott (1771–1832): Scott stopped writing poetry in 1814 and, nostalgic for the virtues of the past, began writing historical fiction that won a wide audience. The best of his so-called "Waverley Novels" and their historical periods are *The Antiquary* (late 18th century), *Old Mortality* (era of the Glorious Revolution), *Rob Roy* (reign of George I), *The Heart of the Midlothian* (age of Queen Anne), *Ivanhoe* (time of Richard the Lionhearted), *Kenilworth* (court of Queen Elizabeth), and *Quentin Durward* (period of Louis XIV).

His characters: Some readers find his heroes and heroines bland, but the villains and minor characters richly drawn. He was particularly adept at creating lively characters from the lower classes.

Theme 8 VICTORIAN PROSE

*T*he Victorian Period was a time of great change as Britain became a major imperial power and the world's first industrialized nation. Steam power, first used to drive industries, also powered fast railways, ships, printing presses, and farmers' combines. These were soon followed by the introduction of the telegraph, intercontinental cable, photography, anesthetics, and universal compulsory education. It was a time of great energy, and the poets and novelists of the period were extraordinarily productive as they sought to chronicle their exciting age and provide it with a high moral tone and a refined taste in literature and the arts. It was also a time of rising unrest, and social consciousness marks much of Victorian literature.

Key 63 Characteristics of the Victorian period

OVERVIEW   *In the early 20th century there was a negative reaction to "Victorianism," which stood for a narrow-minded, prudishly moral, hypocritically religious, and naively optimistic society. Victorian literature suggests that the age was more complex and varied than this.*

Social change: The economic depressions of the 1830s and 1840s led to unrest and demands for reforms in the political system. The working-class Chartist movement demanded equal electoral districts and the right to vote. Reform Bills, beginning in 1832, helped correct the situation. There were outcries against child labor and other industrial problems, and socialism became a political force.

Religious challenge: The Established (Anglican) Church was under fire from several sides. The Oxford Movement questioned its theological legitimacy. The Higher Critics, a group of scholars who studied the Bible textually, challenged the authority of the Scriptures.

Scientific challenge: Another threat to orthodox religion was scientific inquiry, such as Darwin's theory of **evolution** and the geologists' assertion that the earth is milleniums older than the Bible suggests.

The novel: The Victorians' supreme literary achievement was the novel, which was avidly read, with no distinction being made between "popular fiction" and "literature."

Poetry: The most important early Victorian poets were close followers of the philosophy and style of the Romantic poets. All believed that one of the important functions of poetry was to improve the morals of their readers.

Prose: The essays and longer prose works of Victorian writers such as Carlyle, Mill, Newman, and Ruskin had one primary aim: to lead their readers to "superior viewpoints" and improve their taste in art and literature.

Drama: Though the Victorians loved drama, their taste for melodrama and sentimentalism kept the dramatists from reaching the heights of the poets and prose writers. Only Oscar Wilde's satiric comedies of manners are still frequently performed.

Key 64   Major prose writers: Carlyle, Newman, and Mill

OVERVIEW   *Victorian essayists were primarily concerned with a criticism of society's morals, priorities, and tastes. Carlyle emphasized the overall decline of his age. Mill's lucid, more restrained autobiography and essays are classically liberal in philosophy. Newman wrote of religious controversies and new theories of higher education.*

Thomas Carlyle (1795–1881): His unique style used startling shifts in thought, newly coined words, and outrageous metaphors.
- *Sartor Resartus* (1833–34), written as a biography of a fictitious Professor of Things in General, is a diatribe against social conditions. It also relates Carlyle's spiritual journey from negativism to a kind of optimism based on intellectual honesty.
- *On Heroes and Hero-worship* (1840–41) argues that great men make history; historical events do not make great men.
- *Past and Present* (1843) attacks the injustices, materialism, and corruption of the age and calls for a hero to lead England.

John Henry Newman (1801–90): An Anglican who became a Roman Catholic, he strongly opposed religious "liberalism."
- *The Idea of a University* (1852) advocated "intellectual excellence" under ecclesiastical supervision and argued that the purpose of education is to train the mind rather than impart facts.
- *Apologia Pro Vita Sua* ("Explanation of his life," 1864) is an autobiographical work, detailing his spiritual journey, wrestling with theology and his own soul.

John Stuart Mill (1806–73): He precociously studied Greek at age three. Influenced by a Utilitarian father to be agnostic in religion, he became a tolerant liberal.
- *On Liberty* (1859), attacking the loss of freedom of thought, argues that all opinions should be heard because the minority opinion may be true, and even if false may reveal truth more fully.
- *Utilitarianism* (1863) has the main tenet: "Actions are right in proportion as they tend to promote happiness, wrong as they tend to promote the reverse of happiness." Mill's addition to this idea, is his emphasis on the "greatest good for the greatest number."

Key 65 Three major critics: Arnold, Ruskin, and Pater

OVERVIEW *Prose—including novels—was more popular than poetry among Victorians. Essays were avidly read by the middle class, bent on self-improvement.*

Matthew Arnold (1822–88): He judged literature on the basis of three principles: design in the total work, evidence of the elevated ''grand style,'' and a ''criticism of life.''
- *Essays in Criticism, First Series* (1865) includes ''The Function of Criticism at the Present Time,'' with its major premise: that literature criticizes of life, and literary criticism analyzes literature.
- *Culture and Anarchy* (1868) includes ''Barbarians, Philistines, Populace,'' which finds no culture among shallow aristocrats or the survival-seeking poor. He says the Philistines (the middle class) are the only hope.
- *Essays in Criticism, Second Series* (1888) is a selection of his best criticism, including well-known essays on Milton, Keats, Byron, Shelley, and Wordsworth.

John Ruskin (1819–1900): The leading art critic of the century, he strongly identified morality with art in his ornate essays. His later writings focused on social reform.
- *Modern Painters* (5 vols., 1843–1860) promotes the English landscape painters, particularly J.M.W. Turner, and asserts his criteria that great art expresses ''human dignity and heavenward duty.''
- *The Stones of Venice* (I, 1851; II, 1853) promotes the thesis that art is a direct function of national morality.
- *Unto This Last* (1860) marks Ruskin's beginning as a social reformer. He writes that national wealth is a public responsibility to be used for social justice.

Walter Pater (1839–94): Attacking traditional Victorianism and its self-conscious quest for Truth, he advocates Epicureanism, a relishing of the sensuousness of art.
- *Studies in the History of the Renaissance* (1873) exalts Michelangelo because he worked primarily for the joy of creating beauty. Pater stated that art is not the handmaiden of social problems, faith, or morals.
- *Appreciations, with an Essay on Style* (1889) contains incisive essays on Wordsworth, Coleridge, and Lamb.

Key 66   The Victorian novel

OVERVIEW   *No early Victorian author (except perhaps Thackeray) took the novel seriously as an art form, but by 1900 the novel was clearly the era's most distinctive achievement.*

Reasons for the success of the novel:
- Originating as a middle-class genre, it was beloved by the emerging middle-class.
- The novel form was flexible and adaptable to the changes in Victorian life.
- When the Industrial Revolution compounded life's complexities, escapist literature was popular.
- Despite the escapist element, the authors also presented a semblance of reality, appealing to Victorians.
- Novelists gave their readers moral instruction.

Characteristics of the Victorian novel:
- ''Good'' characters are rewarded, ''bad'' ones punished.
- The adjustment of the individual to society is the major human problem presented, with a general acceptance of the values of the middle class.
- The major characters were recognizable Victorian types, with typical aspirations. The poor were usually treated patronizingly, the rich scorned and envied.
- In an era in which human nature is considered basically good, the heroes and heroines are persons of virtue, even though sometimes weak.

Historical novels: Influenced by Scott (Key 62) were Edward Bulwer-Lytton's *The Last Days of Pompeii* (1834) and Charles Reade's *The Cloister and the Hearth* (1861). Major novelists also used the genre: Dickens, in *A Tale of Two Cities* (1859) and Thackeray, in *The History of Henry Esmond* (1852).

Gothic fiction: Rising above the example of Mrs. Radcliffe's tales of terror, Emily Brontë (Key 67) wrote *Wuthering Heights* (1847).

Social romances: Elizabeth Gaskell's *Cranford* (1853), a picture of village life, and **Anthony Trollope's** (Key 69) Barchester novels, which depict the interweavings of clerical and domestic life, are chief examples of this genre.

Key 67   The novels of the Brontës

OVERVIEW   *Three novelist-daughters of a widower-clergyman in Yorkshire presented a thesis never before voiced in English fiction: that a woman's passion and emotional depth can equal or exceed a man's. They were Charlotte, Emily, and Anne Brontë, who, in that chauvinistic age, had to use male pseudonyms to publish Poems by Currer, Ellis, and Acton Bell (1846).*

Charlotte Brontë (1816–55): The eldest, she was the first to write a novel, *The Professor,* but it was not published in her lifetime.

- *Jane Eyre* (1847), the story of a plain-appearing governess who loves a mysterious, Byronic-hero type, Mr. Rochester, was an immediate success because of its emotional and narrative power, delineating elemental life forces. *Jane Eyre* is the most widely acclaimed ''first'' novel in literary history.
- *Shirley* (1849) is a social novel dealing with the industrial conflicts during the Luddite riots and calling for better occupations for women.

Emily Jane Brontë (1818–48): Shy and reserved, she is now considered the genius of the three sisters. She was also one of the most original poets of the century.

- *Wuthering Heights* (1847), now considered one of the greatest English novels, at first met with puzzlement; reviewers dwelled on the morbid aspects of a love story linking Cathy and Heathcliffe beyond death. Her use of natural symbolism makes her a precursor of Thomas Hardy. Her strong characterizations and innovative narrative method in using a ghostly flashback are much praised.

Anne Brontë (1820–49): The youngest sister, she became a governess and used her experiences to write two social romances which some critics think are under-rated.

- *Agnes Grey* (1847) contrasts the gentle nature of a rector's daughter turned governess with the ungovernable children of the upper classes.
- *The Tenant of Wildfell Hall* (1848) was considered morbid because of the character of Arthur, an alcoholic given to wild debauchery (based on the Brontë brother, Branwell).

Key 68   Dickens and Thackeray

OVERVIEW *The era's two most prominent novelists were **Charles Dickens** (1812-1870) and **William Makepeace Thackeray** (1811-1863). Victorian readers loved to weep at the sentiment, laugh at the comedy, and cheer the cries for popular reforms in Dickens's novels. Thackeray, the more consciously artistic, wrote popular novels that contrasted human pretensions and human weaknesses.*

Dickens's early novels: Social criticism here is interlaced with humor.
- *Pickwick Papers* (1836–37), a parody of the picaresque novel, gives a panoramic view of 18th century rural England.
- *Oliver Twist* (1837–39) is a dark melodrama of the crime and squalor of London life, featuring Fagin and his school of young cutpurses contrasted with the pure young Oliver.
- *David Copperfield* (1849–50), Dickens's favorite, is autobiographical and recreates his childhood ingeniously.

Later novels: These works are darker, indicting Victorian society and humanity in general.
- *Bleak House* (1852–53), Dickens's best-plotted novel, shows the effect of a cruel Court of Chancery on English society. Unlike the endings in earlier novels, good does not triumph.
- *Hard Times* (1854), with a relatively small number of characters, attacks industrialism and its ills.
- *Great Expectations* (1860–61), satirizes Dickens's own desperate lower–middle-class passion to rise to gentleman's status.
- *Our Mutual Friend* (1864–65) also satirizes Victorian materialism and the flaunting of wealth.

Thackeray depicted a whole class of English society—the newly elevated middle-class gentry—in minute detail and in a graceful style.
- *Vanity Fair* (1847) introduces Becky Sharp, who violates traditional mores as she acquires wealth and social position.
- *Pendennis* (1848–50) portrays the title character as saved by the pure love of a good woman.
- *The History of Henry Esmond* (1852) has been called the finest historical novel in English. It deals with the love of the chivalrous young hero for a heartless society beauty.
- *The Newcomes* (1853–55) chronicles three generations of a middle-class family eager to rise in class.

Key 69   George Eliot and Anthony Trollope

OVERVIEW   *George Eliot (Mary Ann Evans) (1819– 1880) and **Anthony Trollope** (1815–1882) are studies in contrast. Called the "first modern novelist," Eliot is the earliest English novelist with a massive intellect. She believed in discarding the old concepts of God, faith, and immortality for a "religion of humanity."*

Early Eliot novels: Set in her native Warwickshire, these rustic idylls are her most popular works.
- *Adam Bede* (1859) asserts that love without marriage or marriage without love leads to a wretched downfall.
- *The Mill on the Floss* (1860) is autobiographical; the leading character is the intellectual Maggie.
- *Silas Marner* (1861) is a nearly perfect Eliot novel showing how Marner, a bitter miser, is regenerated by a child's love.

Later novels: These more intellectual novels promote some of her favorite themes.
- *Romola* (1863), set in 15th century Italy, asserts that moral excellence results from incessant good choices.
- *Felix Hall, the Radical* (1866) uses Carlyle's idea that progress comes from spirituality, not politics.
- *Middlemarch* (1871–72) indicts society for not allowing freedom to intellectual and cultural pursuits.

Trollope: The principal conflict in all his major novels is the struggle to retain the old way of life against forces within and outside the middle class. Disciplined in his writing, he placed his watch in front of him and ground out 250 words an hour for four hours each day.

The Barchester novels: Termed "as English as roast beef," these are his most popular works.
- *The Warden* (1855) The hero, the Reverend Mr. Septimus Harding, portrays humble goodness.
- *Barchester Towers* (1857), a sequel, presents all the clergyman types in an age of Anglican church strife.
- *The Last Chronicle of Barset* (1867) presents Trollope's most complex and deeply religious cleric, Josiah Crawley, who is falsely accused of stealing a check for £20.

Key 70 Novelists opposed to
"Victorianism"

OVERVIEW *In the latter part of the Victorian Age, three authors wrote innovative novels that opposed the sentimentality and moral pretentiousness of Victorians with intellectual satire that was less appreciated by their contemporaries than by 20th century readers.*

Samuel Butler (1835–1902): Ripping aside the mask of respectability, he revealed a vision of cruel tyranny and rigid morality in Victorian families.
- *Erewhon* (1872), "nowhere" rearranged, is a scathing reversal of Victorian England.
- *The Way of All Flesh* (1903), an autobiographical novel, was posthumously published. His mouthpiece, Ernest Pontifex, topples the household gods revered by contemporary novelists such as Thackeray.

Lewis Carroll (Charles Lutwidge Dodgson) (1832–98): An Oxford lecturer on mathematics, he vented his anti-Victorianism in ingenious, symbolically complex children's books, now even more appealing to adults.
- *Alice's Adventures in Wonderland* (1865), about a child's falling down a rabbit-hole into a fantasy world, has dream visions and symbolic logic conveying its satire.
- *Through the Looking Glass* (1871) is another dream vision that is even more satirical of the adult world.

George Meredith (1828–1909): An advocate of "advanced ideas," such as woman suffrage, he wrote highly experimental fiction that cost him the appreciation of his contemporaries.
- *The Ordeal of Richard Feverel* (1859) displays Meredith's ironic sophistication and sarcasm in a novel about the love affair of a young man trained from childhood to avoid women.
- *Beauchamp's Career* (1875), Meredith's favorite, is a political novel that takes a hard look at the political and economic problems of the age.
- *The Egoist* (1879), his masterpiece, satirizes the egoism of the Victorian gentleman through his anti-Victorian hero, Vernon Whitford.

Key 71 The novels of Thomas Hardy

OVERVIEW *Thomas Hardy (1840–1928) wrote a long and varied body of major novels reflecting his view of mankind struggling against an indifferent force that rules the world.*

Novels: His affectionate characterization of Dorset villagers is flavored with humor and folklore, and he often reveals his love of the natural world in close detail and with strong symbols. However, his view of life is darkly cynical, and the novels generally end tragically.

Far from the Madding Crowd (1874): A poetic, pastoral epic recounts the love affair between the ruggedly honest farmer, Gabriel Oak, and the volatile Bathsheba.

The Return of the Native (1878): This novel has the tragic intensity of a Greek drama, with characters on brooding Egdon Heath being buffeted by blind chance.

The Mayor of Casterbridge (1884–85): The out-of-work Michael Henchard sells his wife to a sailor; all subsequent action, describing Henchard's rise to mayor and his fall to ruin and death, is colored by that event.

Tess of the D'Urbervilles (1891): This melodramatic novel defied Victorian standards by making a seduced girl the heroine. It was her discovery of aristocratic family connections that led to her downfall.

Jude the Obscure (1895): The furor this novel caused among critics prompted Hardy to turn from writing fiction to poetry. It is literature's most savage indictment of a society that crushes a penniless intellectual, the humble stonecutter Jude. His longing for an education is frustrated and doomed.

Minor novels: Hardy also wrote what he called romances and fantasies—*The Trumpet Major* (1882), a romance set during the Napoleonic wars, and *The Well-Beloved* (1897), in which a sculptor, Jocelyn Pierston, falls in love successively with three generations of women on the isle of Slingers.

Key 72   Victorian drama: Oscar Wilde
and others

OVERVIEW   *The Theater Act of 1843 at last broke the monopoly granted to the Covent Garden and Drury Lane Theaters by the Act of 1737, allowing the modern theater to develop. By 1899 the 61 theaters in London presented mostly melodramas, marked by suspenseful plots, stereotyped characterizations, and sentimentalism.*

Oscar Wilde (1856–1900): He was the spokesman for the Aesthetic Movement ("art for art's sake") with his brilliant wit and conscious posing. His best plays were comedies of manners that were closer to Restoration comedies than to other Victorian plays.
- *Lady Windermere's Fan* (1892) wittily supports the anti-Victorian idea that right and wrong are relative terms.
- *The Importance of Being Earnest* (1895), the most performed drama of the 19th century, uses some of the English stage's most brilliant dialogue to indict trivial, vacuous Victorian upper classes.

Minor dramatists: Important contributions to modern drama were made by playwrights now little remembered.
- **Thomas William Robertson** (1829–71) has been called the first modern British playwright. He introduced the "well-made play" and realistic stage sets and props. *Caste* (1867) explores the problems of marriage between different social classes with eight sharply individualized acting roles.
- **Henry Arthur Jones** (1851–1929) began as a melodramatist and occasionally used sensationalism in his serious plays. *Saints and Sinners* (1884), called the "first serious modern drama," struck out hard against Victorian morality and would perhaps have been run off the stage had not Matthew Arnold defended it.
- **Sir Arthur Wing Pinero** (1855–1934), the best craftsman in 19th century drama, began as a writer of comedies, but he is now remembered for his "well-made" serious plays. *The Second Mrs. Tanqueray* (1893), his best-known work, deals ingeniously with a well-worn question: "Can a woman with a past become respected in polite society?"

Theme 9 VICTORIAN POETRY

*M*ost of the important poetry of the early Victorian period followed closely the style and content of the
Romantic predecessors. Primitivism and revolution were
less accentuated, but the early Victorians were still concerned with the past, particularly the Middle Ages and
ancient Greece. The three major Victorian poets—Tennyson, Arnold, and Browning—came to grips with the religious anxiety and social change of the period. Late Victorian
poets, including Swinburne and the group known as the Pre-
Raphaelites, rebelled against the conventions and traditions
of the earlier poets in a search for freer expression in a somewhat prudish age.

Key 73   The significance of Tennyson

OVERVIEW   *Alfred, Lord Tennyson (1809–92) was the oracle of the Victorian Age, its most popular poet, and the only English author elevated to the rank of Lord for his writings. He was the unfailing voice of orthodox morality, a talented and romantic lyricist, and somewhat of a dreamer and mystic.*

The moralist: Tennyson's beliefs were generally traditional and conservative, though sometimes troubled.
- **"Ulysses"** (1833) glorifies the Victorian drive for fullest achievement, giving it dignity and powerful expression.
- **"Locksley Hall"** (1842) is a dramatic monologue by a disturbed youth whose true love marries into a higher class; to Victorians it spoke of aspirations and confidence.
- *In Memoriam* (1850), an elegy on the death of his friend Arthur Henry Hallam, was a call for strong religious faith, through "honest doubts."
- *Idylls of the King* (1859), blank verse narrative poems about the Arthurian legends, has Arthur represent "the ideal soul of man coming into contact with the warring elements of the flesh."

The romantic lyricist: Tennyson had remarkable metrical facility and made almost musical use of language.
- *Poems, Chiefly Lyrical* (1830) includes the Keatsian earlier lyrics. In "The Poet" Tennyson defines the poet in Romantic terms as the inspirer of mankind to freedom and true wisdom.
- *Poems* (1832) includes some of the best-known poems: **"The Lady of Shalott,"** a medieval allegory; **"The Palace of Art,"** which asks whether the poet should only pursue art or use poetry to help mankind; and **"The Lotos-Eaters,"** a descriptive poem based on an incident in the *Odyssey*.

The morbid mystic: Tennyson's romantic idealism often led him to a despairing view of the present.
- **"The Vision of Sin"** (1832) is a nightmarish dream of being enslaved to vice.
- **"Maud, a Monodrama"** (1855) is a strange, darker "Locksley Hall," with a bitter, love-sick youth becoming insane.
- **"Locksley Hall Sixty Years After"** (1886) is a bitter look back on the blighted love affair. He finds the world of his old age ruined by materialism and liberalism.

Key 74   Robert and Elizabeth Barrett Browning

OVERVIEW   *In 1846, when Robert Browning eloped with Elizabeth Barrett, she was the more famous poet of the two.*

Elizabeth Barrett Browning (1806–61): Kept an invalid by a tyrannical father, she was educated at home. Her verse was appreciated for her pious idealism and zeal for humanitarian reform.
- *The Seraphim and Other Poems* (1838), in the Romantic style, was her first work to gain critical attention.
- *Poems* (1844) contains two familiar poems of social sympathy, "Cry of the Children" and "Cry of the Human." In "Lady Geraldine's Courtship" she alludes to Browning's poetry, leading to their romance.
- *Sonnets from the Portuguese* (1850) is a sonnet cycle about her somewhat maudlin love for Robert.
- *Aurora Leigh* (1851), a 11,000 line "novel in verse" is her masterpiece. It contains witty comments on the position of women in Victorian society.

Robert Browning (1812–89): His reputation grew slowly because his innovative poetry was strikingly different. After unsuccessfully attempting to write dramas and long blank verse dramatic poems, Browning began writing his dramatic monologues. He adopted the "technique of indirection" in his dramatic monologues, showing "Action in Character, rather than Character in Action."
- *Men and Women* (2 vols., 1855), the masterpiece of his middle period, ranged over history, art, philosophy, and religion, and included some of his best poems: "Fra Lippo Lippi," "Andrea del Sarto," "Love Among the Ruins," and "Childe Roland to the Dark Tower Came."
- *Dramatis Personae* (1864), marked by Browning's grief over his wife's death, contains some of his most often anthologized dramatic monologues: "Rabbi Ben Ezra," "A Death in the Desert," and "Caliban Upon Setebos."
- *The Ring and the Book* (1868–69), a blank verse poem in over 21,000 lines, is based on an actual 17th century Italian murder trial. The dramatic monologues vividly portray the characters, as well as the time and setting. The philosophical and religious concerns about "absolute" and "relative" truth are precisely conveyed.

Key 75   The poetry of Matthew Arnold

OVERVIEW   *Matthew Arnold (1822–88) wrote poems portraying intellectuals who feel deeply the loss of traditional faith, then under attack from science, the "higher criticism" of the Bible, and Utilitarianism. His poems show a loneliness and a desperate search for life's meaning and purpose. In his own time, he was the least popular of the three major Victorian poets, but he is now the best-received by 20th century intellectuals.*

"Memorial Verses" (1850): Written on the death of Wordsworth, it sets him, as a poet of feeling, above Bryon, the poet of passion, and Goethe, the poet of thought.

The "Marguerite" poems: "To Marguerite" (1852) and "Isolation" (1855), particularly, show the poet's sense of isolation as he attempts to communicate with his beloved.

"The Buried Life" (1852): This expresses the inability to communicate one's deepest thoughts to another except in rare moments of intimacy.

"The Scholar-Gypsy" (1853): Arnold denounces the intellectual confusion of his age and idealizes a young Oxford student who has "integrity of the spirit" and survives.

"Sohrab and Rustum" (1853): A narrative poem about a Persian hero who unwittingly slays his own son in battle, this was Arnold's most popular poem in its day.

"Stanzas from the Grande Chartreuse" (1855): Written after a visit to the famous monastery, it shows the poet in a dilemma. To him, the old faiths are dead, and modern intellectualism is powerless to replace Christianity.

"Thyrsis" (1866): A pastoral elegy on the death of his friend, the poet Arthur Hugh Clough, it argues that though Clough is gone, his imaginative, creative drive still survives.

"Rugby Chapel" (1867): This is a tribute to the poet's pious father (the Rugby School Headmaster, Thomas Arnold) by an agnostic son.

"Dover Beach" (1867): This poignant lyric reflects the poet's pessimism at the loss of religious faith in his time, ending with a vision of this world as "a darkling plain" on which "ignorant armies clash by night."

Key 76 Pre-Raphaelite poets: Rossetti and Morris

OVERVIEW *In 1848 a group of poets and painters met to form the Pre-Raphaelite Brotherhood, dedicated to carrying on a romantic revolt against academic painting and a return to the clarity, brightness, and fidelity to nature of the paintings before Raphael. They also romanticized the medieval past.*

Dante Gabriel Rossetti (1828–82): Known first as a painter, he had no interest in writing poetry about the political or scientific controversies of the day. He wrote primarily about women and often set his poems in the Middle Ages.
- **"The Blessed Damozel,"** depicting the damozel looking out over the ramparts of Heaven, contains a great deal of medieval sacramental symbolism (three lilies in her hand, seven stars in her hair).
- **"My Sister's Sleep"** is a lyric about the death on Christmas Eve and a sublimating of grief in praise of the newborn Lord.
- **"Jenny,"** a controversial ballad about a prostitute, is the furthest Rossetti went in social criticism.
- **"Sister Helen"** is a ballad set in medieval Scotland. The jilted Helen melts a waxen image of Keith of Ewern, causing him to waste away and die.
- **"The House of Life"** consists of 101 intensely personal sonnets about love, life, and death.

William Morris (1834–96): This early socialist activist was a designer of textiles, wallpaper, and furniture; he also was a painter and poet. All these arts came easily to him, and he frequently wrote poetry in his head while weaving tapestries.
- ***The Defence of Guinevere, and Other Poems*** (1858) is the best single volume of Pre-Raphaelite verse. Almost entirely medieval in subject matter, it includes ballads strongly influenced by Sir Walter Scott.
- ***The Earthly Paradise*** (1868), Morris's longest poetic work, consists of 24 verse tales exchanged by 14th century Viking wanderers.
- ***Sigurd the Volsung*** (1876), showing his interest in Scandanavian literature, is a tragic version of the Siegfried story.

Key 77   Swinburne, antagonist to Victorianism

OVERVIEW   *Algernon Charles Swinburne (1837–1909) revolted sensationally against Victorian religious assumptions and middle-class concerns. His hypnotic poetic virtuosity in every conceivable meter and stanza attracted young rebels of his day, particularly in his poems about freedom.*

Swinburne the Pagan (1860–66)
- *Atalanta in Calydon* (1865) recasts a tale from Ovid into the form of a Greek tragedy. The choruses are superbly melodic.
- *Poems and Ballads* (1866) was motivated, Swinburne stated, by the desire "to be thought an eminent and terrible enemy to the decorous life." Best known is the world-weary lyric, "The Garden of Proserpine."

Swinburne the Freedom Fighter (1866–79)
- *Songs before Sunrise* (1871) is a volume of propaganda poems about freedom and the hatefulness of despotism. The best poem is "Hertha," about the Teutonic earth goddess who symbolizes liberty.
- *Poems and Ballads, Second Series* (1878) follows *Songs before Sunrise* with such similar poems as "A Forsaken Garden" and "Ave Atque Vale" ("Hail and Farewell").

Last years:
- *Heptalogia* ("Seven Jests") (1880) continues his assault on Victorianism with excellent parodies, most notably the ones of Tennyson and the Brownings.
- *Tristram of Lyonesse* (1882) portrays the Tristram-Iseult passionate love affair as a triumph of natural love over Victorian inhibitions.

KEY QUOTATION:

I am tired of tears and laughter,
  And men that laugh and weep;
Of what may come hereafter
  For men that sow and reap:

—from "The Garden of Proserpine"

Theme 10 20TH CENTURY FICTION

*T*wo enormously destructive world wars and the economic disruption of the Great Depression brought to an end
both Britain's colonial empire and whatever remained of the
social and moral certainties of the Victorian era. Freud's
theories of psychology prompted interest in the inner life of
individuals. Technological changes brought great improve-
ments in the physical comfort of life and also attacks on the
materialism and spiritual emptiness of modern life. In all the
arts, this is a period of experiment and innovation. Intellectuals questioned old values in religion and politics with pessimistic results.

Key 78 Characteristics of the Modern period

OVERVIEW *Throughout the 19th century, England was the world's most powerful nation, but the slaughter of World War I shook both the social order and the optimism of the 19th century. The Great Depression and the enormous cost of World War II lowered Great Britain to the status of debtor nation. Unable to maintain its colonial empire, it gave independence to over 600 million people.*

Cultural conditions: Early in the 20th century the revolt against Victorianism continued as intellectuals searched for new answers. To many, religion became unimportant as the British became a secular society, but others, including authors Evelyn Waugh, Graham Greene, and Edith Sitwell, were converted to Roman Catholicism. Others turned to communism, but Stalinist purges of 1936–38 disillusioned most of them. After World War II, intellectuals became the "angry young men" in England, attacking the class system, the Royal Family, the Established Church, and even the London theater. Younger British intellectuals became rudderless, no longer finding comfort in Christianity, Marxism, or psychoanalysis.

Modern literature: Generally, 20th-century writers have been torn between expressing the era's new discoveries and insights (Freudian psychology, for example) and expressing a dissatisfaction with western civilization. Modern writers felt increasingly alienated from the public, and there was a recurrence of ironic, esoteric, and fiercely antagonistic works throughout the period.

Poetry: Pessimism among modern poets embraced two generations: Thomas Hardy and A.E. Housman before World War I, and Wilfrid Owen and T.S. Eliot after. William Butler Yeats, the premier poet of the 20th century, tinged his melancholy with romanticism.

Fiction: In an era of excellent fiction, two of the most significant novelists were not English: James Joyce (Irish) and Joseph Conrad (Polish). Of the other major novelists—D. H. Lawrence, E.M. Forster, and Virginia Woolf—only Woolf lived continually in England.

Drama: After World War II, British dramatists made the greatest impact of all the literary artists. John Osborne (first of the "angry young men"), Harold Pinter, Samuel Beckett, and Tom Stoppard brought important new approaches to the English stage.

Key 79   Social criticism in the Modern novel

OVERVIEW   *Some early 20th-century novelists con-demned the class system, satirized the materialistic acquis-itiveness of all classes, and deplored the terrible conditions of poverty. These novels appealed to middle-class readers.*

John Galsworthy (1867–1933): He received the Nobel Prize for liter-ature in 1932, but has a diminishing reputation. His trilogies about upper middle class families are still highly regarded.
- *The Forsyte Saga* (1922) consists of three novels tracing the for-tunes of three generations of the Forsyte family. Galsworthy, him-self upper middle class, denounces the Forsytes for their narrow minds and consuming desire for wealth.
- *A Modern Comedy* (1929), another trilogy about the Forsytes, now elderly, is more sympathetic.

Herbert George Wells (1866–1946): One of the most prolific English writers, he injected social criticism into his science fiction as well as his novels of lower-middle class life.
- **Bourgeois novels:** Somewhat autobiographical are the comic and realistic early novels *Love and Mrs. Lewisham* (1900), depicting a struggling teacher, and *Kipps* (1905), about an aspiring draper's assistant. His best novel is *Tono-Bungay* (1909), which Wells called "a social panorama in the vein of Balzac." *Ann Veronica* (1909) is a feminist novel about a "New Woman."
- **Scientific romances:** *The Time Machine* (1895) is a social alle-gory set in the year 802701, with society divided into two classes: the subterranean workers, called Morlocks, and the decadent Eloi. *The War of the Worlds* (1898) is a frightening vision of the world invaded by Martians.

Arnold Bennett (1867–1931): Influenced by Balzac and Flaubert, he wrote naturalistic novels about a smug, narrow-minded, lower-mid-dle class, interested only in money and tangible objects.
- *The Old Wives' Tale* (1908), his best-known work, is the classic English naturalistic novel, set in the "Five Towns" of Bennett's Staffordshire youth.
- *The Clayhanger Trilogy*, consisting of *Clayhanger* (1910), *Hilda Lessways* (1911), and *These Twain* (1915) is rich in the sociology of industrial towns and develops the thesis that people are solely what their environment makes them.

Key 80 The fiction of Joseph Conrad

OVERVIEW *Joseph Conrad (1857–1924), born in Poland, learned English late and began writing novels with a cosmopolitan world view, boldly experimental in form and language. Avoiding the conventional problems of other contemporary novels, his themes were universal; he wrote of honor, guilt, and moral ambiguity and alienation.*

Search for technique (to 1904): In this period Conrad experimented with form and language.
- *Lord Jim* (1900), best of the early novels, probes the theme of guilt and atonement in a complex narrative that does not follow a chronological sequence.
- *Youth* (1902), marking the first appearance of Marlow (Conrad's frequent narrator), is a tribute to youth and to unquenchable endurance in a hopeless cause. The volume includes *Heart of Darkness*, the great short novel about the moral disintegration of a Belgian bureaucrat in an African colonial outpost.

KEY QUOTATION

The brown current ran swiftly out of the heart of darkness, bearing us down toward the sea with twice the speed of our upward progress; and Kurtz's life was running swiftly, too, ebbing, ebbing out of his heart into the sea of inexorable time.

—Heart of Darkness

- *Typhoon* (1903), is a powerful tale of a man versus nature during a storm at sea. A man of limited intellect and imagination, but great faithfulness to duty, ultimately wins.

Political and social period (1904–14): Conrad here scrutinized western politics and society and dealt with themes of corruption and human loneliness
- *Nostromo* (1904) has been compared to Tolstoy's *War and Peace* in its stature as one of the world's great novels. Told with an impressionistic technique, this story of an Italian sailor who steals a treasure of silver is also a profound analysis of western capitalism.

- *The Secret Agent* (1907), set in London, castigates science and materialism for hostility to the human spirit. It was suggested by an 1894 attempt by anarchists to blow up the Greenwich observatory.
- *Under Western Eyes* (1911) attempts to explain the nature of Russia to the west in a novel of guilt and atonement.
- *Chance* (1914), the most technically complex of Conrad's novels, treats the emotional isolation of his best-drawn female character.

More conventional technique (1915 to death): Conrad returned to traditional forms at the end of his career.
- *Victory* (1915), his most popular novel, asserts the thesis that western society's moral failures before World War I brought on the holocausts of war.
- *The Shadow Line* (1917), is about a sea captain, becalmed at sea with a sick crew, winning against adversity.

Key 81   The experimental fiction of James Joyce

OVERVIEW *James Augustine Aloysius Joyce (1882–1941), a remarkable combination of realist and symbolist, was a brilliant and rebellious experimenter with the form and language of the novel. He pushed language and linguistic experiment to the outer limits of communication.*

Dubliners (1914): These 15 short stories were intended, Joyce wrote, "to betray the soul of that hempligia or paralysis which many consider a city." In the face of the patriotism of the Irish Literary Renaissance, Joyce depicted Irish degeneration, banality, and tastelessness in such stories as **"The Dead," "Clay,"** and **"Counterparts."**

Portrait of the Artist as a Young Man (1916): This poetical autobiographical novel uses the **interior monologue** (the direct representation of Stephen Dedalus's thoughts). The hero's name combines *Stephen*, the name of the first Christian martyr, with *Dedalus*, the mythical artisan who constructed waxen wings so he could fly out of a labyrinth.

Ulysses (1922): The most controversial literary work of the 20th century, it was censored in America until 1933, in England until 1936. Employing the mythological framework of Homer's *Odyssey*, Joyce uses one day in the lives of three principal characters to portray the universe of human impulses. The inner thoughts of each character are revealed through a **"stream of consciousness,"** with sense impressions from the outer world triggering a free association.

Finnegans Wake (1939): This book is so difficult to read and comprehend that one could spend a lifetime in its study. The principal difficulty is the language; throughout the novel Joyce forces together English and foreign words into one word by using outrageous puns and multiple meanings, e.g., "Oystrygods gaggin fishygods," which suggests *Ostrogoths, oysters, gods, going, gagging* (in the sense of silencing), *fishy* (in the sense of fake), *Visigoths*, and many other possibilities. Finnegan becomes the symbol of all the fallen and resurrected figures of literature and history in this novel that takes all of human history as its subject matter.

Key 82 The innovative novels of Virginia Woolf

OVERVIEW *Influenced by James Joyce and Marcel Proust,* **Virginia Woolf** *(1882–1941) experimented with fiction that ignored plot and discarded conventional characterization. She attempted to explore the inner complexities of experience and probe the intricacies of personal relationships.*

Jacob's Room (1922): Her first stream-of-consciousness novel, it has no plot, but through the thoughts of Jacob Flanders, the inner turmoil of the young is remarkably revealed. Jacob is not a Joycean rebel; he seeks to construct meaning for himself out of the maelstrom of experience around him.

Mrs. Dalloway (1925): Another stream-of-consciousness novel, it experiments with time, blending memory and reality in the thoughts of a fashionable, middle-aged lady during a single summer day.

To the Lighthouse (1927): Considered her masterpiece, it treats one family as a microcosm of all humankind as she plumbs the depths of human experience and such elements as the mystery of personality, the differences between masculine and feminine worlds, and the importance of womanly love to a family. The method is again stream of consciousness.

Orlando (1928): More conventional in narrative form, this is a fantasy of a Renaissance English boy being transformed into a woman. It is suggested that the novel is an allegory of England's change from a masculine-dominated society to a more feminine one.

The Waves (1931): This novel gradually unfolds the consciousness of six characters from youth to age as they search for identity in a machine-age world. The six characters lead rich cultural lives very similar to the author's.

Flush (1932): A fantastic feat of the imagination, it is a biography of Elizabeth Barrett Browning as told from the viewpoint of her cocker spaniel.

Literary Criticism: Virginia Woolf wrote literary criticism that is incisive and well-informed. Most widely read are two series of *The Common Reader* (1925–32).

Key 83   The novels of D.H. Lawrence

OVERVIEW   *David Herbert Lawrence (1885–1930) approached the writing of fiction with religious intensity, using it to reveal the subconscious feelings of human beings. He wrote novels in which the central figure moves from mechanical existence to wholly realized life.*

Autobiographical fiction (1909–12):
- *The White Peacock* (1911), a poetic novel about Lawrence's early life (transported to the middle class), has the lyrical passages about nature that characterizes Lawrence's later work.
- *Sons and Lovers* (1913) compares with Joyce's *Portrait of the Artist as a Young Man* (Key 81) as a poetical autobiographical novel. More realistic than later works, it depicts a sensitive son caught in a conflict between his parents.

Novels of emotional adjustment (1913–20):
- *The Rainbow* (1915), banned upon publication because it examines basic sexual relationships—conventional and otherwise—it is the first half of a family chronicle tracing changing patterns of psychological relationships rather than a merely superfical observation of manners.
- *Women in Love* (1920) continues the family chronicle and defines love as a relationship between ''fulfilled'' persons who retain their selfhood.

Prophetic mysticism (1920 to his death):
- *The Plumed Serpent* (1936) uses symbols from Mexican-Indian rituals to project a jaded modern woman into a state of wholeness, free from civilization's corruption.
- *Lady Chatterley's Lover* (banned in Britain in an unexpurgated form until 1960) is about a love affair between the wife of an impotent aristocrat and a gamekeeper, a dark, sensual, complete man.

Other works: Lawrence produced over a dozen collections of short stories. Some of the best-known stories include *''The Rocking Horse Winner,''* *''The Captain's Doll,''* and *''The Man Who Died.''* Also widely read are such beautiful travel accounts as *Mornings in Mexico* (1927) and *Etruscan Places* (1932).

Key 84   Satirical novelists: Huxley and Waugh

OVERVIEW   *Huxley and Waugh were two of the wittiest commentators on the foibles of 20th century society. Both were intellectuals whose cynicism is set against a wide-ranging knowledge of the arts and the sophisticated life.*

Aldous Leonard Huxley (1894–1963): He has been called an essayist who used the novel as a jesting platform from which to preach his moral ideas.
- *Crome Yellow* (1921), his first novel, is a satire about characters who are spiritually bankrupt. Huxley believes in behavioristic psychology, with the body's biochemistry controlling the mind.
- *Antic Hay* (1923) shows his anger at the modern predicament in a devastating satire about the futile efforts of some dilettantes in science and art.
- *Point Counter Point* (1928), his most experimental novel, derives its technique from music, with themes and counter themes separately developed.
- *Brave New World* (1932), set in the year 632 A.F. (After Ford), has a society in which human beings are mass produced on an assembly line, creating many simple workers and a few intellectuals. It is a horrifying picture, one of the first of the "inverted utopias" in the popular modern genre that includes Orwell's *1984*.
- *Eyeless in Gaza* (1936) experiments with a shifting time and preaches a new mysticism, calling for detachment from the self, the world, and all mankind.

Evelyn Arthur St. John Waugh (1903–1966): He wrote six satirical novels with a wit that rivals Oscar Wilde's as he lays bare the evils of what he considers an artificial, unnatural society.
- *Decline and Fall* (1928) was the first of Waugh's often savage satires.
- *Vile Bodies* (1930), the best of his early satires, has an ingenious levity and lightness of touch as he tells the story of a writer's courtship in which every bizarre mishap imaginable occurs.
- *Brideshead Revisited* (1945) shows the hilarious satirist changed into the Catholic moralist, the primary stance of Waugh's later novels. There is still some surface wit, but he is serious in his theme that it is sin and the world that eventually bring man to God.

Key 85 Critics of society : Orwell and Golding

OVERVIEW *George Orwell (1903–50) and Sir William Golding (1911–) wrote ingenious, widely read novels that painted bleak pictures of the intrinsic cruelty of humans and the terrible effects this maliciousness could cause in extreme bureaucratic societies.*

Orwell (real name Eric Arthur Blair): He wrote several lightly regarded early novels, dealing with his frustrations in a world full of "man's dominion over man," before writing his two major works:

- *Animal Farm* (1945), a satire in fable form about Russian communism, is set on a farm where the pigs revolt against their human masters. The pigs, led by their chief, Napoleon, are corrupted by power, and a new tyranny results. Their slogan is, "All animals are equal but some animals are more equal than others."
- *1984* (1949) is a nightmare novel of a future totalitarian state and one man's hopeless struggle against it. It is a police state completely without privacy, and citizens incur the death penalty for having unorthodox ideas. An official language, "Newspeak," progressively narrows the range of thought. War is a permanent state; Oceania is always in conflict with either Eurasia or Eastasia. Posters everywhere proclaim that "Big Brother is Watching You."

Golding: Awarded the Nobel Prize for Literature in 1983, he has written ten novels in strikingly varied settings, several of them historical. His usual method is to isolate individuals or groups in a desperate situation where humans lose their veneer of civilized behavior.

- *Lord of the Flies* (1954) is his best-known and most typical novel. A group of small boys, isolated on a desert island after a plane crash, quickly fails in an attempt at democracy. Savagery, which in Golding's novels underlies man's true nature, soon takes over.
- *The Inheritors* (1955), another innovative story, tells of a society of cave people being exterminated by a Pre-historic tribe with more brutality and slightly more advanced technology of slaughter.

Key 86   Novelists in search of meaning: Forster and Greene

OVERVIEW   *A group of British novelists, avoiding experimental forms and bitter satire, have written serious novels about characters attempting to find meaning in a chaotic modern world. Forster and Greene have received the greatest acclaim, but other important authors include* **Henry Handel Richardson** *(1870–1946),* **Elizabeth Bowen** *(1899–1973),* **C.P. Snow** *(1905–1980), and* **Anthony Powell** *(1905–   ).*

Edward Morgan Forster (1879–1970): In his early novels, he satirized English travellers abroad and criticized the snobbery of the self-consciously cultured.
- *A Room with a View* (1908) is a comedy of manners, mildly satirical of some self-satisfied English tourists.
- In *Howard's End* (1910), a well-to-do German emigré family clashes with an English family lacking the moral values: "to be humble and kind, to go straight ahead, to love people rather than pity them, to remember the submerged."
- *A Passage to India* (1924), Forster's masterpiece, has the individualism of European culture clash vainly with the depersonalized mystery of India when an Englishwoman falsely accuses a young Moslem surgeon of attempted rape.

Graham Greene (1904–91): His novels, written after his conversion, depict a struggle for grace that frees men from the bondage of sin.
- *Brighton Rock* (1938) is a crime story that introduces readers to Greene's central concept: "the apalling strangeness of the mercy of God."
- *The Power and the Glory* (1940) is set in Mexico at the time of religious prosecution. A "whiskey priest," despite his own sense of worthlessness, resolves to function as a priest until captured.
- *The Heart of the Matter* (1948) depicts the disintegration of Scobie, a deputy police commissioner in West Africa.
- *The End of the Affair* (1951) depicts a wartime love affair in London with supernatural religious overtones.

87 Novelists of the distant past: Graves and Tolkien

OVERVIEW *Graves and Tolkien, who published a variety of literary and scholarly works, are now well-known for their individualistic novels of history and mythology.*

Robert Graves (1895–1985): His works include a frank and powerful autobiography *(Goodye to All That*, 1929) and many volumes of poetry, essays, fiction, biography, and free translations. His historical novels are unusual in their imaginative re-creation of the characters of famous persons.

- *I, Claudius* and *Claudius the God* (both 1934) are narrated by the idiosyncratically conceived persona of the Emperor Claudius.
- *Antigua, Penny, Pruce* (1936) is a barbed tale of sibling rivalry.
- *The Golden Fleece* (1944) is a daring attempt at the re-creation of the story of Jason and the Argonauts, setting it in the primitive cultural era with sudden violence replacing the usual glamorization.

J.R.R. Tolkien (1892–1973): A professor of English Language and Literature at Oxford, he was a well-known scholar for his philological and critical studies. He became internationally appreciated as the author of books of fiction based on a mythology of his own invention. He fashioned an entire primitive world, with its own language and legends, that confronts its characters with many of the same problems our modern era faces. These novels are:

- *The Hobbit* (1937), set in Middle-earth and peopled with men, hobbits, elves, orcs, trolls, and spirits drawn from European folklore, makes a statement against greed.
- *The Lord of the Rings* (3 vols., 1954–55), a sequel, is a mix of history, saga, and poetry as well as philosophy, adventure, and sentiment. Though deriving from the traditional English novel, it is more like a Nordic myth, invented by Tolkien, containing his elves and dwarves.
- *The Silmarillion* (1977), which has an earlier place in the chronology of the stories, was published posthumously. Many consider it inferior to the other works because it contains only high seriousness and seems too concerned with the meaning and coherence of the myths.

88 Masters of the short story: Saki, Coppard, Mansfield

OVERVIEW *The 20th century was a time of great development in the short story. Three excellent practitioners of the art were Saki, Coppard, and Mansfield, who preferred short fiction to novels and who made important contributions to the form and substance of the genre.*

Saki (real name Hector Hugh Munro, 1870–1916): His stories of bizarre humor, tinged with the macabre, satirized upper class conventionality and stupidity. His wit is reminiscent of Oscar Wilde and Evelyn Waugh. A favorite device is to use animals—wolves, tigers, ferrets, bulls—as agents of revenge upon humans. From *Reginald* (1914), his first collection of short stories, to *The Square Egg* (1924), Saki delighted a growing number of loyal readers.

Alfred Edgar Coppard (1878–1957): Poor health terminated his formal education at age nine. He wrote more than 100 impressive short stories in seventeen volumes. His simple country characters are revealed through action, and both comic and tragic portrayals are tinged with poetry. He often shows pity for victims defeated by thoughtless actions and a deep sympathy for the oddities and misfits. His deceptively simple stories are much admired by fellow writers. From his first collection, *Adam and Eve and Pinch Me* (1921), he was encouraged by such literary figures as Ford Maddox Ford.

Katherine Mansfield (real name Kathleen Mansfield Beauchamp, 1888–1923): The first short story writer in English to show the influence of Anton Chekhov, she was increasingly recognized as an original and experimental writer who was interested not in the external world, but in moments of illumination when one learns something about life or selfhood. Her insistence that a short story present a **"slice of experience"** rather than a narrative or moral has greatly influenced later writers. Her stories vary in length from long, impressionistic evocations of family life (''At the Bay,'' ''Prelude'') to brief, incisive sketches (''Miss Brill''). She contributed to the short story genre what Virginia Woolf gave to the novel, using the **stream of consciousness** technique to follow the wanderings of the human mind. She is particularly adept in revealing the thoughts of children. Her best-known collections are *Bliss, and Other Stories* (1920) and *The Garden Party and Other Stories* (1922).

Theme 11   20TH CENTURY POETRY

*P*oets shared many of the preoccupations of novelists throughout this period and were almost uniform in their dislike of contemporary society. Many sought their imagery in the mythology of the past—classical, Celtic, and prehistoric. Most experimented with the formal aspects of verse, employing free verse and unusual metrical patterns in sharp contrast to the traditional metrics and rhyme schemes of the Victorians.

INDIVIDUAL KEYS IN THIS THEME

Key 89   Early Modern poets: Hardy and Hopkins

OVERVIEW   *Thomas Hardy (1840–1928) and Gerard Manley Hopkins (1844–89) greatly affected the course of 20th century poetry, Hardy with his dark themes of human alienation and Hopkins with his innovative techniques.*

Hardy's philosophy: In plainly stated lyrics and biting satires, Hardy conveyed both a pessimistic view of the world and the belief that it could be made better. His function as a poet, he thought, was to bring about improvement by assaulting human cruelty and attacking the "robustious swaggering of optimism," which is "at bottom cowardly and insincere."
- **"Hap"** (1866) expresses a preference for a vengeful god that enjoys human suffering, rather than a system of mere blind chance inflicting pain on humankind.
- **"An August Midnight"** (1899) conveys Hardy's perception that man is an alien in the universe; insects seeking the light on his midnight lamp may be better attuned than man.
- **"The Darkling Thrush"** (1900), set at century's end, has a bird's joyous song give hope to despairing humankind.
- *The Dynasts* (1903–1908) is an epic drama, in 19 acts and 130 scenes, tracing the Napoleonic Wars from 1805–1815.
- **"The Convergence of the Twain"** (1914), on the sinking of the *Titanic,* finds a divine, ironic plan in the tragedy.

Hopkins's technique: His bold poetic devices, verbal eccentricities, obscure imagery, use of words with multiple meanings, and subtle rhythms were so startling that the poems were not published until 1918. He created a flexible meter that he called "sprung rhythm." A Roman Catholic priest, he wrote poems with religious themes.
- **"The Wreck of the Deutschland"** (1876), Hopkins's longest poem, stems from a shipwreck that drowned five nuns.
- **"God's Grandeur"** (1877), a strikingly unconventional sonnet, bemoans the age's loss of contact with nature.
- **"The Windhover: To Christ Our Lord"** (1877), one of the most discussed poems in the language, shows how the most commonplace objects in nature glorify God.
- **"Pied Beauty"** (1877) praises all "dappled things," all things that symbolize Christ's human-divine nature.
- **"Spring and Fall: To a Young Child"** (1880) says that in lamenting the dying year we are mourning our own deaths.

Key 90 Poets of World War I: Brooke, Housman, and Owen

OVERVIEW *The collapse of world order and the brutal mass slaughter in World War I profoundly crushed sensitive British intellectuals who had been nurtured in a post-Victorian world of progress and brotherhood. Of these poets, only Brooke romanticized war.*

Rupert Chawner Brooke (1887–1915): By far the most famous poet of World War I, his five "War Sonnets," which include his famous poem "The Soldier" (beginning "If I should die"), were enthusiastically received, as was the posthumous volume *1914 and Other Poems,* published in 1915. His dazzling reputation survived for many years, but he is now chiefly appreciated for his light verse, such as "The Old Vicarage, Granchester."

A. E. Housman (1859–1936): A classics professor, he wrote poems of flawless economy and grace in the volume *The Shropshire Lad* (1896), the most popular single volume of English poetry for the last 100 years.
- His themes were quietly pessimistic: "Luck's a chance, but trouble's sure"; lovers are false; nature is beautiful, but transitory and unkind; youth will drink, answer the call to war, and die. His "Epitaph on an Army of Mercenaries" has been called the best poem of World War I.
- His best-known poems include "Loveliest of Trees," in which the poet realizes that he has only fifty spring seasons left and must "seize the day" in its natural beauty. Another is "To an Athlete Dying Young," in which the hero dies at a peak moment, preserving his triumph.

Wilfrid Owen (1893–1918): Killed in action a week before the Armistice ended the war, he best expresses the prevailing post-war English sentiment: bitterness about the slaughter, patriotism without sentimentality, and courage in a pointless, chaotic world. He was first revealed to readers in *Poems* (1920), a volume remarkably sophisticated in the use of assonance rather than rhyme. In poems such as "Strange Meeting" (on his sense of kinship with a slain enemy soldier), "Mental Cases" (on the emotional casualties of war), and "Dulce Et Decorum Est" (on the horrors of warfare with poison gas), he made World War I a reality to his readers.

Key 91 The poetry of William Butler Yeats

OVERVIEW *William Butler Yeats (1865–1939) acclaimed the greatest poet since Wordsworth, led the Irish Literary Renaissance of the early 20th century in its turning to Irish myths and folkways for inspiration. Yeat's poetry falls into three distinctive periods.*

The aesthetic period (1889–1910): Yeat's early poetry, influenced by the Pre-Raphaelites and the French Symbolists, has as its main purpose the creation and revelation of beauty.
- *The Wanderings of Oisin* (1899) uses Celtic mythology and has a fairy magic that attracted the poet William Morris.
- *Poems* (1895) uses the symbol of the rose, adopted from Rosicrucian lore, in "The Rose upon the Rood of Time," "The Rose of Peace," and "The Rose of the World" (about his love for Maud Gonne, an advocate of a free Ireland).
- *The Wind Among the Reeds* (1899) is autobiographical, centering on his love for Maud Gonne.
- *In the Seven Woods* (1903) has poems arising from his despair at Maud's marriage in 1903.

The Mask period (1910–25): Now an important public figure, Yeats began writing terser, simpler poems about the realities of the Irish problems. He decided he could best contend by assuming "the mask of some other self," not by escaping into the past.
- *The Green Helmet and Other Poems* (1910) continues to lament the loss of Maud.
- *The Wild Swans of Coole* (1917) moves to a complex cosmographical system. The principal themes are life and death.

The prophetic poet (1925 to death): In his latter years Yeats had a remarkable burst of creative energy that resulted in his best poetry, which was complex, yet realistic and humorous.
- *The Tower* (1928), written out of the fear that the world is approaching the end of a 2000-year-old cycle that started with Christ, contains some of his best-known poems: **"Sailing to Byzantium"** (art can triumph over physical decay), **"Leda and the Swan"** (the rape of Leda by Zeus begins a new world cycle), **"Among School Children"** (a charming contemplation of the nature of being and reality), and the robustly sexual **"Crazy Jane"** series of poems.

Key 92   Eliot and Modernist poetry

OVERVIEW   *T.S. Eliot (1888–1965), an American who became a British subject, was the dominant proponent of "modernist" poetry, which he defined in **The Sacred Wood** and practiced in volumes of poetry that influenced virtually every poet since the 1920s.*

Characteristics of modernist poetry: It condemns modern society, uses complex private symbolism, is purposely difficult, emphasizes tensions, uses freely associated images, employs archetypal symbols and myths, concerns itself primarily with contemporary urban life, and experiments freely with form and techniques.

Eliot's first period (to 1927): The young Eliot produced poems that indicted modern culture, that combined the contemporary scene with subtle allusions from antiquity, and employed ironic satire profusely.

- *Prufrock and Other Observations* (1917), Eliot's first volume, attacks the trivialities of modern life. It includes "The Love Song of J. Alfred Prufrock," about an intellectual trapped in social and sexual failure, and "Sweeney Among the Nightingales," a portrait of the cultureless ape man of modern society.
- *The Waste Land* (1922), most discussed by critics of all 20th century poems, is a condemnation of the sterile futility of modern life. It is esentially a ritual drama with powerful underlying myths.
- "The Hollow Men" (1925) depicts moderns as effigies stuffed with straw.

Second period (1927–1965): When Eliot declared himself "an Anglo-Catholic in religion, a classicist in literature, and a realist in politics" in 1928, he began to replace his cynical skepticism with restrained assertions of hope and faith.

- "Ash-Wednesday" (1930) is the first Eliot poem to be wholly pervaded by Christian acceptance. It is inspired by Dante's *Purgatorio*.
- *Murder in the Cathedral* (1935) is a drama about the spiritual condition of martyrs and those who execute them.
- *Four Quartets* (1943) brings together four complex, multi-level poems previously published in periodicals: "Burnt Norton," "East Coker," "The Dry Salvages," and "Little Gidding." They deal with the nature of art and the revelation of the nature of God.

Key 93   Other Modernist poets: Sitwell and Thomas

OVERVIEW *Dame Edith Sitwell (1887–1964) and Dylan Thomas (1914–53) were involved with innovative groups of poets. Dame Edith was a thorough-going "modernist" and Thomas was an important influence on the New Apocalypse, poets who reacted against the classicism of Auden (Key 94) with turbulent and surrealistic imagery.*

Sitwell's first period (to 1929): Her "non-representational" poetry was influenced by the paintings of Picasso and the Cubists. Poems in *Facade* (1922) reveal a fantastic dream-world, heightened by strange tonal patterns.

Her second period (1929–40): She followed Eliot's path with a savage denunciation of modern society in *Goldcoast Customs* (1929).

Her third period (1940–64): Again she followed Eliot, this time into more traditional religious paths. In *The Shadow of Cain* (1947) she hopes humankind will rise from such inhumane acts as the bombing of Hiroshima to higher planes of love and religious faith.

Thomas: His poetry appealed to the literati because of his surrealistic imagery, but a wide range of readers loved his wild intensity and the excitement generated by his eloquence and energy.
- *Eighteen Poems* (1934) contains "The Force That Through the Green Fuse Drives the Flower," which made him famous. The force that drives external nature also drives human growth and decay.
- *Twenty-five Poems* (1936), in much the same vein as the previous volume, contains "The Hand that Signed the Paper" (condemning tyranny) and "Death Shall Have No Dominion" (celebrating resurrection).
- *The Map of Love* (1939), affected by the beginning of World II and his marriage, is best known for "When All My Five and Country Senses See," about the source of poetic vision.
- *Deaths and Entrances* (1946) has the powerfully religious war poem "A Refusal to Mourn the Death, by Fire, of a Child in London" and "Do Not Go Gentle into That Good Night," a plea for his dying father to resist death.
- *In Country Sleep* (1952) shows a mellower Thomas in the title poem, about a father consoling his daughter about the importance of death in nature's scheme.

Key 94 The "New Signatures" poets: Auden and Spender

OVERVIEW *A group of important English poets in the 1930s were referred to as "New Signatures" poets because their works appeared in a volume of that name. They were greatly influenced by Hopkins, Eliot, and Owen, and they added Marxism to the Modernist creed.*

W.H. Auden (1907–1973): He greatly influenced the succeeding generation of poets, presenting them with a variety of models as he progressed from the didactic, satiric poems of his youth to the complexity of his later work.

British period (to 1940): A prototype of the left-wing intellectual, Auden wrote poems satirizing the middle-class failure to create an ideal communist state.
  * *Poems* (1930) contains the forceful poem "XVI," about the dissolution of modern culture.
  * *Look, Stranger!* (1936, American title: *On This Island*) is the most Marxist of Auden's collections of poetry.
  * *Letters from Iceland* (1936), written with Louis McNeice, contains the witty "Letter to Lord Byron."
  * *Another Time* (1940) contains his majestic tribute to Yeats, "In Memory of W. B. Yeats," and his poem on the beginning of World War II, "September, 1939."

American period (1940–73): The communist ideal is replaced by the position of the Christian intellectual.
  * *The Double Man* (1941, English title *New Year Letter*) describes the "baffling crime" of "two decades of hypocrisy."
  * *For the Time Being: A Christmas Oratorio* (1944) was dedicated to his devout Anglo-Catholic mother.
  * *The Age of Anxiety: A Baroque Eclogue* (1948), opening in a New York bar, reflects humankind's isolation.

Sir Stephen Harold Spender (1909–   ): Once more popular than Auden, he has been called the "modern Shelley" both for his liberalism and his lyricism. From 1953–1967 he was the editor of *Encounter*. Much of Spender's best poetry contemplates the difficulties of the machine age. "The Express," a glorification of the beauty of the steam locomotive.

Key 95 Poets of "The Movement": Larkin, Fuller, Davie

OVERVIEW *A group of young poets influenced by Eliot and Auden were given the label "The Movement" in a 1954* Spectator *article. Their poetry was characterized by a conversational style, allusions to everyday trivia, disillusionment with a seemingly mad world, and extensive self-scrutiny. Unlike the New Signatures poets, they had no interest in politics.*

Philip Arthur Larkin (1922–1985): The best known of the group, he has been termed Auden's successor. Though he lacks Auden's range and versatility, he is a more disciplined craftsman.
- *The Less Deceived* (1955) brought Larkin immediate acclaim. The poem "Church Going," about a skeptic in an era of little faith wandering sensitively through an old church, is the major example of "Movement" verse.
- *The Whitsun Weddings* (1964) enhanced Larkin's reputation with poems that satirize the pointlessness of urban and suburban life, but show a stoic acceptance of it.
- *High Windows* (1974) is preoccupied with death and the transience of life.

Roy Broadbent Fuller (1912–   ): He is a bridge between the New Signatures poets of the 1930s and the Movement.
- *Poems* (1939) shows the influence of Auden and Spender.
- *The Middle of the War* (1942) is the best volume of war verse from World War II.
- *Collected Poems* (1962) indicates no belief in immortality or hope for the human situation, but counsels endurance and dignity. In "To Posterity" and in "Expostulation and Inadequate Reply" Fuller views humankind as a dying species on a doomed planet, but his imagery has a somber grandeur. His work is often compared to the poems of Hardy.

Donald Davie (1922–   ): His poems are speculative, philosophical, and erudite. His mind, as he says, "moves most easily and happily among abstractions." His poems reflect his extensive travel, and he strongly rejects English provincialism. His volumes show an admiration for 18th century poetry and an extensive grasp of history.

Key 96 Traditional poets: Blunden, Muir, and Betjeman

OVERVIEW *Amid the volatile environment of changes in style and technique fostered by the Modernists, the New Signatures poets, and the poets of the Movement, there were those who wrote traditional poems in styles that seemed idiosyncratic to the avant garde.*

Edmund Charles Blunden (1896–1974): He wrote poems about the English countryside and rural life with precise natural imagery. His poems about his World War I experiences reveal feelings of guilt about his own survival.
- From *Poems* (1914) through *After the Bombing* (1950) to *A Hong Kong House* (1962), he speaks of war's assault on nature and paints compelling portraits of the country women and men who people his landscapes.

Edwin Muir (1887–1958): A quietly optimistic poet, he thought the powers of good (which were closer to elemental simplicity) were greater than the powers of evil. He was more interested in myths and archetypal symbols than in the problems of the contemporary world.
- *Collected Poems 1921–58* (1960) typically contains imagery rooted in the landscapes of childhood. A recurrent theme is a dream journey through time and place.

John Betjeman (1906–1984): Named poet laureate in 1972, his work has reached an unusually wide public while also gaining the appreciation of fellow poets Auden and Larkin. His poetry is primarily witty, urbane, and satiric, but there is also an underlying melancholy and a religion based more on hope than faith.
- *Collected Poems* (1958) has sold more copies than any volume of poetry since Tennyson. Larkin said of it that Betjeman writes as though "all modern literature since the 1920s never existed." Betjeman satirizes the welfare state and is nostalgic for pre-1914 England.
- *Summoned by Bells* (1960), the first volume of a projected blank verse autobiography, covers his boyhood and life at Oxford.
- *A Nip in the Air* (1972) and *High and Low* (1976) appealed to a new generation of admirers who replaced those who had drifted away in the late 1950s, thinking Betjeman too facile of phrase and too popular as a public figure to be a great poet.

Theme 12   20TH CENTURY
DRAMA

*D*rama in the modern era moves from the realism and naturalism of the early part of the century—itself a rebellion against Victorian conventions—to the theater of the absurd and the experimental drama of the contemporary stage. Social and political criticism is a major preoccupation throughout the period.

Key 97   Shaw: Major dramatic influence

OVERVIEW   *George Bernard Shaw (1856–1950) advocated replacing light, artificial dramas with plays depicting social and moral problems in the mode of Henrik Ibsen.*

Ideas: A free thinker, Shaw supported women's rights, equality of income, abolition of private property, and a change in the voting system. His plays are witty discussions, with conflicts of ideas rather than of neuroses and physical passions. In his more than 50 plays he sought to provoke his audiences intellectually by making them laugh.

Early dramas: More durable than the later, more important plays, the early dramas followed Ibsen in presenting social criticism in "**well-made**" plays, but relied greatly on Shaw's distinctive wit.
- *Mrs. Warren's Profession* (1894) was not produced until 1902 because the "profession" is prostitution, and the theme is that virtue is impossible in a capitalistic society.
- *Arms and the Man* (1894), an anti-war play, burlesques the idea of military heroism.
- *Candida* (1894), Shaw's favorite, has a love triangle of a successful clergyman, his lovely and intelligent wife, and an 18-year-old poetic genius.

Later plays: In the period from 1901–29, Shaw achieved his greatest creativity. He was still preaching, but was free of Ibsen's methods.
- *Man and Superman* (1901–03) remakes the Don Juan legends in modern guise and argues that progress only comes through transforming human nature.
- *Major Barbara* (1905) has a brilliant conflict between a ruthless entrepreneur, Lord Undershaft, and his daughter, an idealistic major in the Salvation Army.
- *The Doctor's Dilemma* (1906) shows skepticism about the medical profession.
- *Pygmalion* (1912) satirizes British social classes and language in a play that was remade as *My Fair Lady*.
- *Back to Methuselah* (1921), a complex philosophical drama, requires three nights to perform.
- *Saint Joan* (1923), Shaw's last great drama, portrays the world's treatment of a young genius ahead of her time.

Key 98   Shaw's contemporary
dramatists

OVERVIEW   *While Shaw dominated the English stage there were four other relatively minor playwrights—Galsworthy, Granville-Barker, Barrie, and Maugham—who were contributing to the scope of drama in London's West End with plays that were individualistic, yet influenced in varying degrees by Shaw.*

John Galsworthy (1867–1933): Also prominent as a novelist, he began his theatrical career with *The Silver Box* (1906), a play about a theft using his favorite device of parallel families, one rich and one poor. *Strife* (1909), an investigation of industrial managers, and *Justice* (1910), in which a minor felon is crushed by the judicial system, are his best works.

Harley Granville-Barker (1877–1946): A brilliant actor-director at the innovative Royal Court Theater, he made a lasting impact on English drama by producing works of Shaw and Galsworthy, along with his own plays. *The Voysey Inheritance* (1905) is a realistic play with the theme that one's private moral responsibility supersedes public moral responsibility. *Waste* (1907) is a powerful tragedy about an idealistic politician destroyed by scandal.

Sir James Matthew Barrie (1860–1937): He is perhaps best known for his whimsical children's play *Peter Pan* (1904). Still frequently performed is *The Admirable Crichton* (1914), in which a shipwreck allows a butler to become the leader of a family of inept aristocrats. *Dear Brutus* (1917) is a fantasy about guests who enter a magic "Wood of Might Have Been" to discover their other possible fates.

W. Somerset Maugham (1874–1965): Perhaps better known as a novelist, he wrote five plays that display a superb ear for witty dialogue and the ability to craft ingenious "well-made" plays. *Our Betters* (1917) satirizes title-hunting Americans, *The Circle* (1921) cleverly shows elopement as the death of romance, *East of Suez* (1922) spectacularly evokes street scenes in Peking, *The Constant Wife* (1926) depicts a wife's cunning revenge on an unfaithful husband, and *For Services Rendered* (1932) is a bitter anti-war play.

Key 99   Irish playwrights: Synge and O'Casey

OVERVIEW *John Millington Synge (1871–1909), a leading figure in the Irish Literary Renaissance, wrote one of the 20th century's great tragedies as well as one of its great comedies. Another strongly nationalistic Irish dramatist whose plays were produced at Dublin's Abbey Theater was **Sean O'Casey** (1880–1964), rated by some critics as second only to Shaw among 20th century playwrights.*

Synge's plays: In his best plays Synge mirrors the gullibility, superstition, and brutality, as well as the innate charm, of the Irish peasantry. His language is enriched with the rhythms and diction of peasant speech.

- *Riders to the Sea* (1903) is an elemental tragedy of death and resignation in a fisherman's family, set on the west coast of Ireland.
- *The Playboy of the Western World* (1907) caused wild riots as Irishmen considered themselves maligned by Synge's comedy about a son's revolt against his father.
- *Deirdre of the Sorrows* (1910), unfinished at Synge's death, brilliantly tells an ancient Irish legend in modern Irish speech.

O'Casey's plays: Also tied strongly to the life and language of the Irish poor, O'Casey's plays bring together the tragic and comic.

- *Juno and the Paycock* (1924), set in 1922 during the civil war between the Irish Free State and the Irish Revolutionary Army, shows the disintegration of the Boyle family.
- *The Plough and the Stars* (1926), set during the Easter Rebellion, portrays tragicomically eight separate defeats for eight characters.
- *Within the Gates* (1933) is the first fully expressionistic O'Casey drama and is therefore highly stylized and abstracted (like a morality play, Key 15). The theme is the conflict between the repression of life and the celebration of life, a recurrent problem, inherent in the Irish character and personality.
- *The Stars Turn Red* (1940) was attacked in Ireland as Communist propaganda. The message is more liberal than radical, but the unfortunate title suggested otherwise.

Key 100   Beckett, dramatist of the absurd

OVERVIEW   *Samuel Beckett (1906–1989), born in Ireland of Jewish parentage, moved to France in 1932 and wrote his remarkable dramas in French, translating them into English himself. The leading proponent of the "Theater of the Absurd," he revolutionized drama in England and deeply influenced young dramatists with his innovative use of the stage and his new approach to symbolism.*

Waiting for Godot: First staged in French (1935), it received resounding acclaim in its first English performance at Cambridge (1955). Two tramps are endlessly waiting for the arrival of the mysterious Godot, engaging in bouts of witty wordplay. Pozzo arrives, driving the rope-bound Lucky with a whip. With this scant action and few characters, Beckett powerfully and symbolically portrays the human condition as one of ignorance, delusion, and paralysis, enlightened rarely by flashes of hope and human sympathy.

Endgame (1958): A one-act drama, it features the irascible, senile Hamm, his attendant Clov, and Hamm's "accursed progenitors," who reside in trash-cans.

Krapp's Last Tape (1959): In this monologue, the aged Krapp tries to rekindle his earlier feelings by listening to recordings of his younger self.

Happy Days (1961): Winnie, buried to her waist in a mound, is still attached to the precisely catalogued contents of her purse.

Come and Go (1967): A minimalist play, it has three female characters and a text of 121 words.

Breath (1969): This 30-second play consists of only a pile of rubbish, a breath, and a cry.

Not I (1973): A short, fragmented monologue is delivered by an actor of indeterminate sex and of whom only the mouth is illuminated.

The novels: The last important works Beckett wrote in English were the novels *Murphy* (1938) and *Watt* (1942–44, 1953). These indicate a strong influence from James Joyce and Franz Kafka and, in their bold experimentalism, exemplify the "novel of the absurd" just as *Waiting for Godot* is a prime example of the "theater of the absurd."

Key 101 Contemporary British dramatists

OVERVIEW *The dramatists generally considered to be the most important on the present-day London stage are coincidentally those who were most influenced by Beckett and the Theater of the Absurd. In plays by Pinter, Stoppard, and the South African playwright Fugard, however, there is a more positive underlying ethical purpose, not merely a symbolic portrayal of a fragmented, disintegrated society.*

Harold Pinter (1930–): He is known for his "Pinteresque" style of dialogue which realistically reproduces the nuances of conversational speech, with its pauses, silences, and difficulties in communication. His frequent themes include jealousy, family hatreds, mental aberrations, and erotic fantasies.
- *The Birthday Party* (1958) portrays an out-of-work pianist in a seaside boarding house being threatened by two mysterious intruders.
- *The Caretaker* (1960), a complex, enigmatic play with dialogue that is both naturalistic and surreal, depicts the interaction of three characters: the brothers, Aston and Mick, and a tramp named Davies, whom Aston rescues from a brawl.
- *The Homecoming* (1965) is a dark, erotic, Freudian drama of a son's bringing his wife into the womanless household of his father and brothers. She calmly accepts their sexual overtures and rejects her husband.
- **Other plays** include *Old Times* (1971), *No Man's Land* (1975), and *Betrayal* (1978).

Tom Stoppard (1937–): He has a biting wit, particularly in word-play, a strong sense of theatrical possibilities, and great inventiveness in the structure of plays. His dramas pose ethical problems and, realistically, do not always offer a solution.
- *Rosencrantz and Guildenstern Are Dead* (1966), his second play, attracted much attention for the device of making the "attendant lords," Rosencrantz and Guildenstern, central to his play. There is verbal wit, Shakespearean parody, and a tragic sense of the lack of mastery over one's destiny.
- *Jumpers* (1972) reveals the principal character, a professor of moral philosophy, through lengthy speeches that are brilliant parodies of academic philosophy.

- *Travesties* (1974) is set in Zurich, where Lenin, James Joyce, and a minor historical figure named Henry Carr resided during World War I. Joyce and Carr appeared in an amateur performance of *The Importance of Being Earnest*, and Stoppard builds this actual incident into an extravaganza of witty commentary on Joyce's *Ulysses* and Lenin's politics, as well as a parody of Wilde's play. One scene is written entirely in limericks.
- **Other plays** include *Dirty Linen* (1976), on parliamentary misdemeanors; *Every Good Boy Deserves Favor* (1977), about a dissident in a Soviet mental hospital; and *The Real Thing* (1982), a marital tragi-comedy.

Athol Fugard (1932–): A South African playwright, he has stunningly revealed the problems of *apartheid* among various ethnic groups in his country. His use of symbols is akin to Beckett's, whose work he admires.
- *The Blood Knot* (1961) is about the relationship of two brothers, designated "colored" in South Africa.
- *Boesman and Lena* (1968) has a homeless, middle-aged couple set up their shelter on the open stage, suggestive of Beckett.
- *A Lesson from Aloes* (1980) contrasts the political attitudes of an Afrikaner, his wife, and their "colored" friends.
- *Master Harold . . . and the Boys* (1982) tellingly depicts the relationship between a white South African teenager and two black family servants.

GLOSSARY

absurd

Literature or drama that has as its basic premise the meaninglessness of life in the 20th century; it uses banal repetitions and fantasy.

Alexandrine

A line of poetry with six iambic feet, used by Spenser as a long ninth line in his Spenserian stanza.

allegory

A narrative poem or prose work in which persons, events, and objects stand for something else.

alliteration

The repetition of initial sounds in a series of words in poetry or prose.

allusion

A reference in a literary work to a famous person or event in history, the Bible, a literature, or mythology.

analogy

The comparison of one object, condition, process, or event to another in order to clarify or intensify the image or thought.

archetypes

Those images which are a part of the collective subconscious of all humanity.

ballad

A poem that tells a story, often of folk origin, usually in four line iambic stanzas with the second and fourth lines rhyming.

baroque

A style in art, architecture, literature, and music characterized by flamboyancy, elaborate ornamentation, and a symmetrical arrangement.

blank verse

A type of poetry in which rhyme is not used. Each line has ten syllables with an iambic rhythm.

bombast

Inflated, extravagant speech, found in many Elizabethan poems and plays.

carpe diem	A Latin phrase, meaning literally "seize the day," first used by Horace and applied to lyric poems that have the theme "Eat, drink, and be merry, for tomorrow we may die."

classicism	The philosophy of art associated with the ancient Greeks and Romans, typically characterized by balance, moderation, self-control, dominance of reason, and respect for tradition.

closed couplet	A pair of rhymed lines of poetry containing a complete statement.

comedy of manners	A type of satirical comedy, especially popular in the Restoration and Neoclassical periods, concerned with the manners of a highly sophisticated and artificial society and characterized by witty dialogue.

convention	A literary practice, style, or technique that has become, through frequent use, an accepted method of literary expression.

couplet	Two rhyming lines of poetry, usually in lines of eight or ten syllables each.

cycle	A term—which originally meant "circle"—used to describe a collection of poems or romances, as in "sonnet cycle."

decadence	A term used by literary historians to denote the decline that signals the end of a great period in literature, characterized by such qualities as abnormal and artificial subject matter, extreme self-consciousness, and overly subtle style.

didactic	A term used to describe poetic works whose primary objective is to teach or to convey moral observations.

elegy	A long and formal poem meditating on the dead; often written to commemorate the death of a fellow poet.

129

end-stopped line	A line of poetry in which the idea is complete and which ends with a punctuation mark.
epic	An extended narrative poem, written in an elevated style, recounting the deeds of a legendary or actual hero.
essay	A prose composition, usually brief, dealing with a particular theme or topic.
expressionism	A literary movement of the early 20th century, found mostly in drama, dedicated to revealing the depths of the human mind (after the discoveries of depth psychologists like Freud). Expressionist theater uses unreal atmospheres, distortion, and stylized action to depict external representations of extreme psychological states.
fabliau	A short comic tale in verse, often coarse in content, popular in French literature of the 12th and 13th centuries and the form used by Chaucer in several *Canterbury Tales*.
farce	A type of low comedy with broad and obvious humor and much physical action.
free verse	Poetic compositions in which there is neither rhyme nor a regular meter; also called *Vers libre* (French for free verse).
genre	A term used to indicate the various categories in which literary works are grouped by form; from the French word for kind or type.
gothic novel	A type of novel, first popularized in the late 18th century, characterized by thrill-provoking and supernatural events.
grotesque	When applied to literature, the word has come to denote characters who are spiritually or physically deformed.
heroic couplet *130*	A pair of rhymed lines written in iambic pentameter.

Horatian ode	An ode in which each stanza follows the same metrical pattern.
imagery	A term used frequently in literary criticism to refer either to figures of speech or to verbal representations of sensory objects or sensations.
informal essay	An essay that is usually brief and has a purpose that is less serious than a formal essay.
interior monologue	A technique used in the writing of a novel or short story to record the inner thoughts and emotional responses of a character; also called stream of consciousness.
irony	A rhetorical device in which the author conveys a meaning opposite to the words actually used.
Italian sonnet	Also called the Petrarchan sonnet, it is divided into an octave (eight lines), which always rhymes *abbaabba*, and a sestet (six lines), which rhymes cdecde.
kenning	A type of phrase found in Old English poetry as a figure of speech to stand for a simple noun, as in *whale road* for sea.
lyric	A short, melodic, imaginative poem, usually characterized by intense personal emotion.
melodrama	Although the term literally means "a play with music," melodrama today denotes a play with stereotyped characters and highly charged emotions, usually with a romantic plot and a happy ending.
metaphor	A figure of speech implying a comparison between objects of different classes or categories by saying one object *is* another, not *like* another.

miracle play	A type of drama, common in medieval England, that depicts a miracle performed by a saint, or an incident in the life of one. These plays are not usually based strictly on scriptual accounts.
mock epic	A long poem, intended to be humorous, that treats a trivial subject in the lofted, exalted style of the epic poem.
morality play	A type of drama, popular in medieval England, characterized by a pronounced use of allegory to point up a moral teaching.
mystery play	A type of medieval play based on Biblical stories.
myth	Stories that come anonymously from the remote past; myths stir the subconscious in powerful ways because such folklore and folk beliefs are based on a kind of primitive truth that once attempted to explain inexplicable psychological and scientific truths to ancient ancestors.
naturalism	A type of realistic fiction that developed in France, America, and England in the late 19th and 20th centuries. It presupposes that human beings are like puppets, controlled completely by external and internal forces.
Neoclassicism	A term used to describe a set of literary characteristics that flourished in the age between the Restoration (beginning in 1660) and the publication of *Lyrical Ballads* (1798), which signaled the triumph of Romanticism in English literature. Neoclassical literature is characterized by an emphasis on correct form, wit, common sense, elegance, reason, and a careful control of the emotions.
octave	A poetic stanza with eight lines, now used chiefly to denote the first eight-line section of an Italian sonnet.

ode	A sustained lyric poem with a noble theme and an intellectual tone.
ottava rima	A poetic stanza with eight iambic pentameter lines rhyming *ababababcc*.
pastoral	A poem about shepherds and rural life, derived from ancient Greek poetry.
parody	A humorous literary work that ridicules a serious work by imitating and exaggerating its style.
pentameter	A line of poetry containing five metrical feet.
persona	In the criticism of fiction, the term refers to a person through whom the narrative is told.
personification	A figure of speech that gives human forms and characteristics to abstractions, ideas, animals, and other creatures.
point of view	A phrase used in literary criticism to denote the vantage point from which an author presents the action in a work of fiction.
prosody	A word applied to the theory and practice of writing poetry.
quatrain	A stanza or poem with four lines, with many possible rhyme schemes.
realism	A term generally applied to any literature that is true to life. It is specifically applied to a movement in the latter half of the 19th century, when novelists were reacting against Romanticism.
refrain	A regularly repeated phrase or line of poetry that recurs frequently in a poem or ballad.
rhyme	A similarity or correspondence in the vowel sounds of two words that have differing consonantal sounds.

rhyme royal   A type of stanza containing seven iambic pentameter lines and rhyming *ababbcc*.

rhyme scheme   The recurring pattern in which rhymes are placed in a stanza or poem.

romance   Originally a term denoting a medieval narrative in prose or poetry, dealing with a knightly hero; but now, any fiction concerning heroes, exotic subjects, passionate love, or supernatural experiences.

run-on line   A line of poetry in which the sense of the sentence or clause is not completed (as in an end-stopped line) but which continues into succeeding lines.

short story   A brief narrative, ancient in origin, which includes fables, parables, tales, and anecdotes.

soliloquy   A monologue delivered by an actor alone on stage.

sonnet   A poem of 14 iambic pentameter lines with a rigidly prescribed rhyme scheme. The two main types of sonnets the Italian (or Petrarchan) and the English (or Shakespearian).

Spenserian stanza   A nine-line stanzaic form consisting of eight iambic pentameter lines followed by an Alexandrine, a line of six iambic feet.

stanza   A group of lines of poetry arranged as a melodic unit that follows a definite pattern.

subplot   A secondary dramatic conflict that runs through a story as a subordinate complication and which is less important than the main plot.

symbol   Something that is a meaningful entity in itself and yet stands for, or means, something else.

terza rima   A special type of three-line stanza that has inter-locking rhymes in a continuous rhyme scheme: *aba bcb cdc ded*, etc.

tone   The author's attitude toward his subject and his audience as implied in the literary work; for example, a *satirical* tone.

tragedy   A serious drama, in prose or poetry, about a person, often of a high station in life, who experiences sudden personal reversals.

tragic irony   A form of irony that occurs when a character in a tragedy uses words that mean one thing to him and something more meaningful to the audience.

tragi-comedy   A type of drama that is initially serious in tone or theme, until it becomes apparent that the tragic events will end happily rather than with a catastrophic event.

unities   Principles of structuring dramas requiring that the plot be one continuous action (unity of action), that the action takes place within the walls of one city (unity of place), and in one day (unity of time).

verse   A general name given to all metrical (or poetic) compositions.

INDEX